making unity more visible

fig.1
Statue of
Dietrich
Bonhoeffer on
the west portal
of Westminster
Abbey.
Sculpted by
Tim Crawley.

making unity more visible

the report of the
Meissen Commission,
1997–2001

the Church of England and the
Evangelical Church in Germany

CHURCH HOUSE
PUBLISHING

Church House Publishing
Church House
Great Smith Street
London
SW1P 3NZ

ISBN 0 7151 5765 5

Designed by Visible Edge

Typeset in Franklin Gothic 9.5/11

Printed by Halstan & Co Ltd,
Amersham, Bucks

Published 2002 by Church House
Publishing

*Copyright © The Archbishops' Council
2002*

GS Misc 654

contents

Illustrations

preface

At the end of the year 2001, the Meissen Agreement between the Church of England and the Evangelical Church in Germany (EKD) reached the end of its second five-year period. During this time our two Churches have moved forward in many areas of fellowship and collaboration, both within our own countries and as part of worldwide ecumenism.

Meissen has given a major stimulus, in terms of theological dialogue and as a practical example of how churches can work together in common mission, to many other ecumenical initiatives over recent years. But Meissen itself continues to enrich the mission of the Church in our two countries, as the contents of the present report testify.

The pages that follow reflect the commitment of local parishes and dioceses, theologians and Church leaders, of sector ministries and educational institutions, to participate in Meissen in increasingly fresh and inclusive ways, drawing our Churches together towards the closer unity envisaged in the first report published in 1997.

The commission's report was finalized in September 2001, and is signed by its co-chairmen, Dr Hans Christian Knuth, the Bishop for Schleswig, and Bishop Michael Bourke of Wolverhampton. Bishop Knuth retired as co-chairman of the commission at the end of 2001. I should like to express deep gratitude on behalf of the Council for Christian Unity for his commitment and tremendous enthusiasm for Meissen during the ten years of his work in this role.

The report has been considered by the Council for Christian Unity on behalf of the Archbishops' Council, endorsing the recommendations for the work of the commission during the next five years. Readers new to Meissen will find copies of the original Declaration and the Implementation Agreement in the appendices, along with reports from the last two theological conferences. The reports reflect the views of those who participated in the conferences; their publication in this report does not necessarily imply that those views are shared in every detail either by the commission or by the Council for Christian Unity.

The Council for Christian Unity commends the report of the Meissen Commission to members of the General Synod, and hopes that it will be welcomed by them and more widely within the Church of England. I hope that the report will inspire new areas in which our Churches can work together and meet the challenges of this new century in living out the gospel in our two nations. Comments on the report would be welcomed, and should be sent to the Revd Dr Charles Hill at the Council for Christian Unity, Church House.

On behalf of the Council

✠ Ian Petriburg

Chairman, Council for Christian Unity
April 2002

foreword

Spanning the beginning of the new millennium, the last five years have seen sunshine and shadow, and ongoing achievements as well as some disappointments, in the work of the Meissen Commission.

Bishop Gordon Roe, the first Anglican co-chairman of the Meissen Commission and one of its founding fathers, sadly died only three years after his retirement. July 2000 saw the death of Robert Runcie, whose determination as Archbishop of Canterbury to contribute towards the reconciliation of our Churches and our countries was one of the chief inspirations behind the Meissen Agreement. May they rest in Christ's peace, and rise in glory.

One of the principal hopes set out in the Meissen Agreement is that our two Churches will be able to resolve the outstanding difference between us of the historic episcopate, in order to achieve full interchangeability of ministries. Two further theological conferences have been held on this subject in the last five years, which are reported on more fully in the body of this document. The papers from the conferences, which will be published, have greatly improved our mutual understanding and sympathetic appreciation of each other's histories and theologies. We have, however, had to recognize that it is not possible at the present time to resolve this remaining difficulty. Nevertheless, at the practical level, mutual exchanges of ministers are now possible through the application of the Local Ecumenical Partnership (LEP) model to English and German parishes. We hope that this will open up a new era of mutually enriching experience in the years to come.

Theological conversations and official exchanges cannot convey the sense of excitement and warm human friendship that are the human realities accompanying all the contacts between our Churches. Partnerships between parishes, dioceses and Landeskirchen continue to flourish. New discoveries are made about evangelization, education, ethics and social responsibility in our shared European context. Church members and leaders alike are constantly surprised by the outpouring of generous hospitality, love and humour in all our encounters. The annual meetings of the Meissen Commission itself are no exception to this. As co-chairmen we are deeply grateful for the wonderful spirit that has characterized our sessions, and the enthusiasm with which all the members of the commission have shared in the work together. We wish to record our thanks especially to the co-secretaries and to mention the outstanding contribution of Dr Colin Podmore, the English co-secretary who served the commission with distinction until he took up another appointment in 1999. In all these ways we have the sense of being guests together at God's feast of good things. It is vital that this work continues as we seek the full visible unity of the body of Christ.

Hans-Christian Knuth, Bishop for Schleswig
Michael Bourke, Bishop of Wolverhampton

Co-Chairmen, The Meissen Commission

postscript

At the end of this second five-year period Bishop Hans-Christian Knuth is stepping down as German co-chairman, and this is another milestone on our journey. We express our gratitude to him for the loving dedication that he has brought to the work of the commission during the first ten years of its life, providing leadership, continuity, and above all the sense that our work is rooted in love for Christ, his gospel, and his one Church which manifests itself in our distinctive cultures and traditions. Witnessing more effectively to that unity-in-diversity is our continuing task.

Michael Bourke

introduction

tribute to Bishop Gordon Roe and Archbishop Robert Runcie by Bishop Hans-Christian Knuth

We owe the Meissen Declaration to decisive initiatives taken by the Archbishop of Canterbury, Dr R. A. K. Runcie. In his speech during the debate in the General Synod of the Church of England in London on 9 November 1988, he recalled first the horrific *Kristallnacht* of 50 years before, when in Nazi Germany the terrible persecution of the Jews reached a first horrifying climax. The archbishop recalled, however, how at this dark hour there was also the friendship between Bishop Bell and 'Germans of another hue', in particular Dietrich Bonhoeffer. Bonhoeffer used his last words before he was executed to send a message to Bishop Bell and, as the archbishop underlined, 'Since then there has been a steady stream of members of the Church of England and the German churches who have maintained these bonds of living communion, not least with the Church in East Germany.'

The second basis the archbishop offered for the acceptance of the Meissen Declaration was his own experiences during his visits to East and West Germany, especially on the occasion of the celebration of the 500th anniversary of the birth of Martin Luther in 1983. The archbishop emphasized what we held in common in our liturgical tradition and practice, in our faithfulness to the Scriptures in matters sacramental, in our choral and organ music and in our music for congregational use, but above all in our common call to faithfulness in the face of the secular world.

The archbishop's third reason for proposing the acceptance of the Meissen Declaration was that the relevant sections of canon law permit such ecumenical partnerships. There were, he said, already some concrete areas in which the Church of England was in close community with the Churches in both East and West Germany, even if at present they were still to be realized fully. The archbishop closed his speech with a report on the origins of the Meissen Declaration. He recounted how during the Luther year he had expressed in Leipzig the hope that the fellowship between the three Churches might be deepened. He had ended his participation in the Luther year with a visit to Dresden where he had remembered the terrible Allied air raid as well as, naturally, the German bombing of Coventry. In his speech in the Kreuzkirche he had spoken about reconciliation between Germany and Great Britain and also between East and West in a divided Europe.

The beautiful order for the Communion service had been sung by the choir of the Kreuzkirche and had been very similar to that contained in the 1662 Book of Common Prayer. At the end of the service, as he was distributing communion, he encountered some young Germans who, at some danger to themselves, were bearing peace banners and expressed their thanks to him that he was playing his part in breaking down the barriers between peoples. The archbishop expressed the hope that both past and present in the life of the Churches in England and Germany should come together to make the adoption of the Meissen Declaration possible.

After the Meissen Agreement was signed, Bishop Dr Gordon Roe, as Chairman of the English committee, began to put it into practice. Bishop Roe spoke fluent German. He had studied French and German literature and was a qualified linguist. As co-chairmen, he and I set about at the same time establishing a partnership between our own churches; we were thus able to put into effect at the local level between North Elbe and Ely what we were encouraging at national level. Bishop Roe very quickly won the hearts of his partners. His wonderful sense of humour was an expression of his trust in God which also manifested itself at times when his health was causing him problems. After two life-threatening heart operations he even undertook, with me, the stresses and strains of leading a German–English delegation to southern China to renew our joint Anglican and North Elbian leprosy mission. A high point of this journey was a visit to the senior bishop, Bishop Deng.

Bishop Roe spoke at seven big events organized by the North Elbian church to mark the 50th anniversary of the end of the Second World War. Above all, at a service attended by hundreds of schoolchildren he did not pull his punches in recounting his terrible experiences with Germans in his own childhood. That meant it was even more impressive for the young people to discover how in the course of our lives our perspectives can change when reconciliation and our willingness for peace are allowed free rein. In the midst of the controversy surrounding the dedication of the memorial to 'Bomber' Harris, Bishop Gordon was very concerned that the German side should not have a false impression of this undertaking.

The North Elbians loved this gentle bishop. He often preached to them, often administered Holy Communion to them. The door to Bishop's House was always open and he and his wife, Mary, always offered a warm welcome. This sense of fellowship and welcome was experienced by many sisters and brothers, not just in the partnership between Ely and North Elbe, but also in the relationship between the EKD and the Church of England. Through him we all felt touched by God's good Spirit. A portrait of him has pride of place in the EKD headquarters in Hannover.

fig.2 The Dresden Orb and Cross, made by Grant Macdonald of London.

chapter 1

implementation of the commitments of 1991 and the recommendations agreed in 1996

meetings of the commission

The Implementation Agreement provided that the commission should 'towards the end of each five year period . . . review the progress the churches have made during that period on the way to full visible unity, and their fulfilment of the pledges they have made' (para. 19). Members of the commission were appointed for five years, from 1991 to 1996 and again from 1 January 1997 to 31 December 2001.

At its first meeting in 1991, the sponsoring body decided to call itself 'The Meissen Commission', this name being short and the same in both languages. In order to reflect its tasks in its name, the commission also agreed the following 'long titles': 'The Meissen Commission – The Sponsoring Body for Church of England–EKD Relations' and 'Meissen Kommission – Arbeitsausschuss für die Beziehungen der EKD zur Kirche von England'.

For the period 1996–2001, the Archbishops of Canterbury and York appointed the following Church of England members:

> The Rt Revd Michael Bourke (Bishop of Wolverhampton; Co-Chairman)
> The Revd Dr John Kelly (to 2000)
> Mrs Tonie Smith, JP
> The Revd Peter Townley
> Dr Natalie Watson (from 2001)
> The Venerable Colin Williams

The EKD Council appointed the following EKD members:

> Bischof Dr Hans-Christian Knuth (Bishop for Schleswig; Co-Chairman)
> Pfarrer Christoph Hellmich
> Frau Ursula Köhler

Dr Alfred Rauhaus

Pfarrer Dr Christof Theilemann

The following served as co-secretaries:

Oberkirchenrat Paul Oppenheim (Kirchenamt der EKD)

Dr Colin Podmore (Assistant Secretary, The Council for Christian Unity) (to 1999)

The Revd Dr Charles Hill (European Secretary, The Council for Christian Unity) (from 1999)

The following were invited to the meetings of the commission as observers without a vote:

Pfarrer Dr Uwe Vetter from London, as the representative of the Evangelische Synode deutscher Sprache in Grossbritannien

The Revd Martin Reakes-Williams from Leipzig, as the representative of the Anglican Episcopal Churches in Germany

The Revd Canon John Lindsay, Scottish Episcopal Church (SEC) Europe Group (1999)

Mrs Norma Higgott (SEC), as the representative of the Celtic Churches (from 2000)

As provided for in the Implementation Agreement (para. 17), the annual meetings of the full commission were held alternately in England and Germany, using the language of the host country for both the proceedings and the minutes.

The full commission has met as follows:

11–15 September 1997	St John's College, Durham
17–21 September 1998	Mauritius-Haus, Niederndodeleben, Magdeburg
16–20 September 1999	Hengrave Hall, Suffolk
14–18 September 2000	Predigerseminar, Nürnberg
13–17 September 2001	Lancaster Hall Hotel, London

An important part of the meetings is the twice-daily worship, including the Eucharist and prayers, according to the rites and traditions of the two Churches.

The English and German committees have also met separately between meetings of the full commission, two or three times a year.

The commission's English committee is a committee of the Council for Christian Unity, which receives the minutes of both the committee and the commission. It is responsible to the Archbishops' Council of the Church of England. The German committee reports to the EKD Council.

the Celtic Churches

Following its first five-year report, an invitation from the Meissen Commission for representation from the Scottish Episcopal Church (SEC), the Church in Wales and the Church of Ireland had been welcomed, but in view of the strain on the resources of these smaller Churches it was agreed to appoint a single Celtic Churches representative who would report back to the Conference of Celtic Bishops.

As these Churches, along with the Church of England, are signatories of both Porvoo and Reuilly, the commission wished them to be part of the ongoing discussions between the EKD and the Church of England.

The commission agreed to welcome a Celtic representative, and at the meeting of the commission held at Hengrave Hall in 1999, the Revd John Lindsay of the SEC Europe Group was present. However, in Nürnberg in 2000, Mrs Norma Higgott of the SEC was welcomed as the representative of the Celtic Churches.

partnerships

The Meissen Declaration envisaged that one of the main engines driving the implementation of the Meissen process would be the development of partnerships between Church of England dioceses and EKD Landeskirchen. It was envisaged that from those partnerships would grow links between deaneries, parishes and cathedrals, as well as between those engaged in sector ministries who would enter into partnerships with their opposite numbers in their partner diocese/Landeskirche. The Implementation Agreement provided that 'such partnerships shall involve visits and exchanges

3

of lay people and ministers (whether in groups or as individuals), exchanges of information, shared worship, prayer and spiritual reflection and joint discussions about matters of common concern'.

The development of such links has been one of the successes of the Meissen process. As at September 2001, some 15 diocesan partnerships are now known to be in existence, with 4 other links involving the see city or principal city of the diocese but not having the status of diocesan links, as well as several other notable links between individual deaneries, and many individual parish links.

Partnerships between dioceses and Landeskirchen have produced a rich variety of activity. During the last five years, for example:

- The long-established **Coventry–Dresden** link, a powerful symbol of reconciliation whose potency extends beyond the relationship between Britain and Germany, has expanded to take in parishes from Kenilworth. This culminated in a visit from Dresden to Kenilworth in 1999 in which the concept of shared mission was explored.

- A process of 'shadowing and sharing' has been developed as part of the link between the **Diocese of Ely** and the **Nordelbische Kirche** whereby a German pastor shadows an English priest for a few weeks and vice versa. This has been developed beyond the parish situation so that, for example, the Ely and Nordelbische ecumenical officers are in close touch.

- The link between **Propstei Magdeburg-Halberstadt** and the **Diocese of Worcester** was evaluated and then renewed in 1998. This led to the drawing up by two representatives from each Church of a mission statement which has won formal approval from both Churches. The review also led to a new method of working. Each member of the Worcester Steering Group is given a particular area of responsibility and works closely with his/her opposite number in Magdeburg to develop that area.

- The link between the **Diocese of Blackburn** and the **Braunschweig Landeskirche**, first entered into for a period of five years in 1996, was evaluated and then renewed for a period of ten years during 2001. A feature of the link has been the close relations that have developed between those working with children and young people in Blackburn and Braunschweig. This has led to shared training conferences in Blackburn and Braunschweig for those involved in nurturing faith in young children. It has also led to participation by young people from Blackburn in the annual Braunschweig Confirmation Camp.

- In December 1999, the Bishops of **Berlin-Brandenburg** and **London**, Bishop Dr Wolfgang Huber and the Rt Revd Richard Chartres, signed an agreement establishing the partnership between the Evangelische Kirche in Berlin-Brandenburg and the Diocese of London. Since then, to the satisfaction of all, the agreement has resulted in a wide variety of contacts between parishes and sector ministries in both churches. Contacts in the area of youth work and parish work have been especially intensive. Beyond this, efforts are being made to develop continuing cooperation and joint action in the areas of church music, church schools and chaplaincies (to hospitals, the police and prisons). Over and above this, two conferences – held in London in May 2001 and in Berlin in October 2001 – have taken place in which both churches met together and discussed how the Church can develop an authentic role in its ministry to cities. In autumn 2000, the title of Honorary Canon of St Paul's Cathedral was conferred on Bishop Huber in London. The title of *Ehrendomprediger* was conferred on the Bishop of London in Berlin Cathedral in November 2001. The Meissen Commission has strongly encouraged the establishing and the development of this important link.

    One of the signs of increasing warmth in the partnerships between individual dioceses and Landeskirchen is the number of invitations issued by partners to be present at significant events in each other's life. As four out of many examples:

- In the context of the partnership between the Diocese of Ely and the Church of the North Elbe, representatives from North Elbe were present at the farewell service for Bishop Stephen Sykes and at the requiem service for Bishop Gordon Roe. The Church of North Elbe is also represented each year at the Petertide ordinations. The Diocese of Ely has in turn been represented at the installation of the new Bishop of Holstein-Lübeck and the installation of new deans (*Pröpste*) in Hamburg and Husum, as well as at the Advent ordination in Schleswig Cathedral.
- The Diocese of Worcester always issues invitations to its partner church in Magdeburg to significant events in its own life. Two representatives from Magdeburg will be attending the Worcester Diocesan Assembly at Swanwick in February 2002.
- Individuals from Blackburn and Braunschweig are always present at each other's ordination services. Individuals from Braunschweig have been invited to be present at the installation of the Bishops

of Burnley and Lancaster. A group of Braunschweig clergy attends the triennial Blackburn diocesan clergy conferences.

- In May 2001, the service of enthronement of the Rt Revd John Hind (formerly Bishop of Gibraltar in Europe) as Bishop of Chichester was attended by senior representatives of the Evangelical Church of Berlin-Brandenburg and the Kirchenkreis Bayreuth in Bavaria.

Partnerships between deaneries have been a feature of the developing Meissen process. The partnership between the Deanery of **Salford** and the Propstei of **Lünen** has grown more ecumenical in nature over the last five years, drawing in Roman Catholic (on both sides), United Reformed Church and Free Evangelical Church involvement.

Most of these partnerships are served in the Church of England by a links officer, often supported by a committee. In Germany there is a contact person for each partnership, who acts as a link to the Kirchenamt of the EKD. During the last five years consultations have been held for these links officers and contact persons in England and in Germany, attended by the chairmen or officers of the Meissen Commission. These have been very useful in sharing information, promoting the Meissen process, and strengthening the motivation and enthusiasm of those immediately responsible for developing our partnerships at the practical level.

An information pack, produced during the first quinquennium, has been revised and is available for anyone interested in partnerships or exchanges. This may be obtained from the European Secretary, Council for Christian Unity, Church House, Great Smith Street, London SW1P 3NZ.

ministerial exchanges in Local Ecumenical Partnerships (LEPs)

A significant development for the interchangeability of ministries has been the decision of the commission to apply the model of the English Local Ecumenical Partnership (LEP) to relationships between suitable German and English parishes.

Without this special provision, clergy exchanges are governed (on the Anglican side) by Canon B 43. This permits non-Anglican clergy to officiate in Anglican churches in a number of ways, and offers more opportunities for ecumenical exchange than many parishes are aware of. The Meissen Commission therefore encourages all parishes and dioceses to make maximum use of Canon B 43, which is all that is required for many visits and exchanges, and which requires very little by way of special agreements or permissions.

Canon B 44 is designed for those situations where there is a greater and more long-term commitment to joint worship, mission and ministry. It applies, by definition, to situations which are the exception rather than the rule, and where an LEP can be established within the context of a special covenant for unity.

LEPs require the approval of the bishop of the diocese and of the parochial church council. Canon B 44 cannot therefore be applied to the whole partnership between an Anglican diocese and a Landeskirche. But, within the context of such a partnership, particular local twinnings between parishes can be declared to be LEPs, allowing a greater degree of ministerial exchangeability than is otherwise possible. English Church lawyers advise us that the word 'local' in the title 'Local Ecumenical Partnership' is intended to be interpreted broadly: thus, the churches involved do not have to be located in the same geographical area, and LEPs can be formed out of sector ministries as well as congregations.

Proposals for such an LEP model have been approved by the Meissen Commission, and by the House of Bishops, and the EKD and its member Churches are being informed about them. They entail the following provisions:

- The identification of pilot parishes or sector ministries (such as university and prison chaplaincies) in England and Germany where there is already a history of close cooperation, and which might be ready for an exchange of ministries in an LEP context.
- The establishment of a sponsoring body representing the authorities of the Landeskirche and the diocese.
- The formulation of a declaration of intent and a constitution for the LEP by the sponsoring body. The declaration of intent should include a commitment to joint prayer, mutual visits and common forms of mission and evangelism which can be realistically tackled together (see Appendix H for a model covenant and guidelines on a constitution, which can be used in framing proposals for individual LEPs).
- The constitution should provide a framework for joint worship and sacramental life. One of the most sensitive issues in the Meissen context is confirmation, which is performed by the bishop in the Church of England and by the parish pastor in the Churches of the EKD.

- The constitution should also lay down guidelines for ministerial exchanges and appointments. Under Canon B 44 German pastors can be appointed to assist in the cure of souls in Church of England parishes, and can be paid from the Diocesan Stipends Fund. They can have de facto pastoral responsibility for a congregation (though they cannot be in sole charge); and they can preside at the Eucharist regularly, provided that there is 'Anglican provision' on certain major festivals.

- Joint decision-making in such an international LEP would be in the hands of a local partnership group consisting of members of each Church, and in contact with the ecumenical officers of the diocese and the Landeskirche. The local partnership group should meet at least once a year, and report to the sponsoring body.

- The sponsoring body is responsible for resolving theological and practical difficulties which arise in the partnership, and for instigating a thorough review every seven years.

The Meissen Commission will encourage the development of these LEPs, in the first instance by identifying one or two pilot examples to test the guidelines. The commission will **provide training**, especially for the members of sponsoring bodies, and encourage the participation of theological teachers and students to maximize our investment of theological and ministerial expertise in this particular form of the search for fuller visible unity. The English and German secretaries of the Meissen Commission will act as LEP advisers to fulfil these objectives. It will be particularly important for the Meissen Commission to receive and evaluate the seven-year review reports.

Such LEPs fall short of the full interchangeability of ministries that our Churches seek. Nevertheless they represent a significant step forward, and have been welcomed as such especially by the German members of the commission. We know of one Anglican priest who is working as a pastor in a German congregation in the Church of Baden. This illustrates the fact that, at present, Anglican clergy are eligible for appointments in German Landeskirchen, whereas German pastors can work in the Church of England only under the provisions of the ecumenical canons, as described above.

training

The 1996 report stated that our Churches have a great deal to learn from each other in the sphere of formation and post-ordination training, but reported that 'little progress has been made'. It recommended that the necessary material and financial arrangements should be made for the exchange of ordinands and probationary ministers (Vikare/Vikarinnen).

A number of exchanges have continued to be organized by **colleges, courses and other training schemes**. Queen's College, Birmingham, and the West Midlands Ministerial Training Course enjoy a significant group exchange with the theological faculty in Leipzig, alternating each year and lasting about a week. Another series of week-long visits has been successfully organized between Westcott House in Cambridge and the training department in the Evangelische Kirche von Kurhessen-Waldeck.

There are regular training exchanges within some **partnerships between dioceses and Landeskirchen**: for example, between Hereford and Nürnberg, between Braunschweig and Blackburn, and between Chichester and northern Bavaria. Here a 'Feuerstein Conference' is held every two years which brings together Anglican curates, Lutheran Vikare/Vikarinnen and Roman Catholic seminarians and curates from the Archdiocese of Bamberg. Perhaps the most extensive developments have taken place between the Nordelbische Kirche and the Diocese of Ely, with regular reciprocal visits between German and English curates, and a month-long programme of 'Shadowing and Sharing' between English parish priests and German pastors. The Meissen Commission believes that these partnerships provide the best context for exchanges of those in training and in curacies, and that more initiatives should be taken at this level. However, it is helpful for the Meissen Commission to be kept informed.

During these five years the commission has heard of 13 German probationary ministers who have spent time in a wide variety of contexts in the Church of England: in parishes, cathedrals, youth work and university chaplaincies. We also know of other students who, having completed their first theological examination, have spent a year in an English parish while waiting for a place in the *Predigerseminar* to continue their training. The commission values the interesting reports it has received from some of these people. A German studying in Durham has contributed a valuable MA dissertation on Anglican defences of the historic episcopate.

Guidelines have been drawn up for the care of German Vikare/Vikarinnen whilst in Church of England parishes.

During the same period, the commission has knowledge of only one English ordinand who is undertaking part of his training in Germany, alongside specialist theological research. This disappointing imbalance is due partly to the low number of German-speaking English ordinands, and the Meissen Commission publicizes courses and funds which are available to improve linguistic proficiency, for example those provided by the Goethe Institut and the Ecumenical Study Centre at the University of Bochum. A medium-level proficiency in German (such as Stage 2 of an Open University course) is necessary for participation in a German-speaking exchange.

A further reason for the relatively low number of English participants is the difficulty of fitting extended periods of study abroad into the syllabus of ordination training in English theological colleges. To address this, representatives of the Meissen Commission have held consultations with the Ministry Division, with the House of Bishops, and with the principals of the theological colleges and courses. These conversations have raised awareness of the possibilities of study in Germany, and of the scholarships available from the Council for Christian Unity and the EKD. As a result of these conversations, we are aware of current interest among a small number of students and staff in one or two colleges.

The commission has also asked diocesan directors of ordinands to encourage suitable students to spend time in Germany during a gap year between university and theological college.

A more fruitful approach in England is probably to use the opportunities of continuing ministerial education (CME). Conversations have been held with diocesan directors of CME, to explore the possibilities of the fourth year of first curacies. This is probably the nearest the Church of England can come to the well-established pattern of the *Auslandsvikariat* (curacy abroad) in the EKD. Other CME-based opportunities are offered by sabbaticals in a German parish, university or college. We know of some sabbatical exchanges, and of *Pastoralkollegien* (in-service training colleges) in Germany which offer attractive courses.

Additional publicity about all these forms of exchange has been included in the information pack. The commission is therefore able to report increased efforts in this area, but limited success; and we would like to challenge the English theological colleges and the Ministry Division to adopt new ways of encouraging English students to draw on the strength of theology in Germany.

We recommend that meetings be arranged in each country for those who have taken part in student exchanges of any kind up to the present time, so that the experiences gained can be shared and reflected upon.

libraries

One of the steps agreed in the Implementation of the Meissen Agreement was that the Church of England and the EKD should help each other to establish a library of Anglican studies in Germany and a library of German Protestant studies in England.

In Germany, the University of Tübingen maintains a collection of theological literature in English and German which specializes in Anglican studies. The commission regards this as fulfilling the commitment expressed in the Meissen document.

In England, a new Meissen Library was opened in Durham on 2 December 1998 by His Grace the Archbishop of York.

The library, which is owned and maintained by Durham Cathedral, is housed on the ground floor of the deanery. It was formally established by an agreement between the EKD and the Dean and Chapter of Durham dated 10 December 1997.

The library currently contains more than 30,000 volumes, of which the larger part from the redundant *Predigerseminar* in Imbshausen is a gift from the Landeskirche of Hannover. Much material was also given by the *Kirchliches Aussenamt* of the EKD in Hannover through the good offices of Bishop Heinz Joachim Held and OKR iR Klaus Kremkau, both of whom also contributed generously from their own libraries. A number of other individuals have also given books and periodicals.

The work of preparing the rooms and providing shelves was assisted by grants from the Dean and Chapter, the St Augustine Trust, SPCK and the Kelham Theological College Fund. Much of the work of unpacking, shelving and cataloguing was undertaken by the Canon Librarian, Professor David Brown, Professor Ann Loades and Mrs Anneliese Arnold, assisted by student volunteers. The Meissen Commission is deeply indebted to the North Elbian Church and to Annkatrin Kolbe, an ordinand from the North Elbian Church, who has assisted with the computerization of the catalogue, which through integration with the catalogue of Durham University Library will greatly increase the usefulness of the library to scholars.

The library is used mainly by research students. It is particularly useful to German scholars who would otherwise be deprived of ready access to works they would expect to find in a university library at home. One Norwegian scholar immediately found on the open shelves a book for which he had been touring libraries in continental Europe in vain. The main room also provides a quiet haven for authors; the first whole book to be written there has recently been published. Access to the Meissen Library is through the Deanery Chapter Library.

So far about 200 boxes of books have been shelved; over 100 remain to be opened. £70,000 is needed in order to extend the library into the mediaeval undercroft of the Prior's Chapel, to make it damp-proof and to provide shelves.

The Meissen Commission will explore sources of further funding for this work and will also publicize the library and its contents more widely in England.

theological conferences

Following the Meissen Declaration (B §1), two 'official theological consultations' had already taken place prior to 1996, 'Koinonia and Eucharist' in 1995 in Berlin, and 'Episcope in History, Theology and Praxis and the Future We Share' in 1996 in West Wickham.

The Meissen Commission was able to publish the papers presented in West Wickham in 1997 through Church House Publishing, the official publishing house of the Church of England, under the title Visible Unity and the Ministry of Oversight. Most of the German contributions, translated into English by Dr Colin Podmore, appeared in both languages.

Following the recommendations of the report of the Meissen Commission, two further theological conferences were held during this quinquennium, from 10 to 15 March 1999 in Springe, near Hannover, and from 14 to 19 March 2001 in Cheltenham. Both conferences were jointly chaired by Prof. Dr Ingolf Dalfeth and the Bishop of Stafford, the Rt Revd Christopher Hill.

The delegates to the West Wickham conference had pointed out in their concluding document that we need to clarify what we mean by 'full visible unity', and in what way this goes beyond the kind of relationship we already have. As a result, the Springe conference took as its task the discussion of the 'unity we seek'. The positions presented at Springe and the discussions based on them achieved an important clarification which was summarized as follows:

> In this context we understand the striving for 'full visible unity' not as the attempt to add something to the unity already given by Christ which is visible in Word and Sacrament, but as the struggle of our Churches to witness to this unity in a more comprehensive way and to correspond to the promise contained in it more faithfully.

For the EKD this statement means that the goal of 'full visible unity' expressed in the Meissen Declaration is compatible with the concept of ecclesial unity of the Leuenberg Concord.

The Theological Commission of the EKD produced a statement regarding Church unity which was ratified by the Council of the EKD in autumn 2001 and published in the series of *EKD Texte* as *Kirchengemeinschaft nach evangelischem Verständnis* (*The Protestant Understanding of Ecclesial Communion*). This text explicitly refers to the dialogue with the Church of England and cites the final declaration of Springe. We can therefore say that the impetus of Meissen has contributed to the process of clarification of the theological position of the EKD with regard to ecclesial unity and communion.

At Springe, observers from other Churches were invited for the first time (see Appendix F) and given the opportunity to present their own positions. Following a recommendation from the commission, the Secretariat of the Leuenberg Commission was invited to participate and was represented by President Dr Wilhelm Hüffmeier.

The Cheltenham conference, entitled 'Ten Years On. Ways Forward from Meissen', discussed the Leuenberg ecclesiological text *The Church of Jesus Christ*. The conference also studied the Church of England text *Bishops in Communion*. The participants attempted in their contributions to apply the terminology of the Leuenberg text to the relationship between the EKD and the Church of England in a constructive way. Taking up the distinction made by the Reformers between the foundation and the shape of the Church, it was affirmed that

> in acknowledging 'one another's churches as churches belonging to the One, Holy, Catholic and Apostolic Church of Jesus Christ and truly participating in the apostolic mission of the whole people of God' (Meissen 17 A (1)) we recognize that this one foundation is present in our respective churches in different shapes.

The conference concluded from this that 'it would not be right for one church to require the other to adopt its own ordering of liturgy, ministry, and church government'.

With regard to the question of the ordained ministry, the conference delegates discovered 'a number of common features which reflect the same underlying theological principles'. These include 'a common intention in ordaining ministers of Word and Sacrament', 'an ordered transmission of authority', 'the office of personal oversight in its varying descriptions and the conferring of this office in a liturgical act including prayer and the laying on of hands'.

Agreement about the historic episcopate, which from an Anglican point of view remains the essential prerequisite for the full interchangeability of ministers, has not yet proved possible. Nevertheless, the Springe and Cheltenham conferences achieved a better understanding of why, on the one hand, Anglicans value the historic succession as a sign (but not guarantee) of the apostolic succession of the whole Church; and why, on the other hand, the German Churches, having given up the historic episcopate at the Reformation, learnt to value their own succession in the apostolic faith and their own ministerial continuity as fully adequate. The two conferences explained and reaffirmed the mutual recognition by our Churches of each other's ministries, including those that exercise *episkope.*

The results of the theological conferences encouraged the EKD and the Church of England to continue to work towards

- deeper theological agreement in our understanding of the ministry and ministries (i.e. the ministry in its relation to the royal priesthood of the baptized, the nature of the diaconate, and the issue of the 'threefold ministry');
- developing various forms of collegiality in the exercise of all forms of oversight (visitation, confirmation, ordination);
- considering the practice of confirmation within the communion of our Churches;
- theological reflection on our Churches' mission to our societies in the European context, including the theological foundations and criteria of our engagement with ethical problems;
- interchangeability of ministries in the context of our shared future.

consultations and delegations

meetings of bishops and Church leaders

The Meissen Commitments include invitations to bishops and other senior clergy to share in the meetings of the House of Bishops or its equivalent in each other's Churches. In June 1998 Bishop Axel Noack, the Bishop of the Church Province of Saxony, attended the House of Bishops' meeting in Liverpool. In January 2000 the Rt Revd Michael Bourke, the Bishop of Wolverhampton, was invited to the conference of German Church leaders and their spouses in Chorin (east of Berlin), which was addressed by Herr Günther Verheugen, the German Commissioner responsible for the enlargement of the European Union.

delegation visits

delegation visit to the Diocese of Blackburn, 9–14 February 2000

From 9 to 14 February 2000, a third delegation visit of Church leaders from the EKD and the Church of England took place in the Diocese of Blackburn, in the north-west of England. The topic of this visit was 'Passing on the Faith to the Next Generation'.

The participants from the EKD were:

The Chairman of the Council of the EKD, Präses Manfred Kock (Düsseldorf)

Bishop Dr Hans-Christian Knuth (Schleswig), Co-Chairman of the Meissen Commission

Bishop Dr h.c.Rolf Koppe, EKD Central Office, Hannover

Dipl.-Päd. Elke König (Greifswald)

Prof. Dr Manfred Kwiran (Wolfenbüttel)

Oberkirchenrat Dr Michael Trensky (Karlsruhe)

Together with Oberkirchenrat Paul Oppenheim, EKD, Hannover.

The Church of England delegation comprised:

The Archbishop of York, the Most Revd Dr David Hope

The Bishop of Blackburn, the Rt Revd Alan Chesters

The Rt Revd Michael Bourke, Bishop of Wolverhampton and Co-Chairman of the Meissen Commission

Mrs Margaret Behenna (Exeter) and Mr Stuart Emmason (Manchester), members of the General Synod of the Church of England

Canon Vivienne Faull (Coventry)

Mrs Elizabeth Paver (Sheffield), member of the Archbishops' Council

The Ven. Colin Williams, Archdeacon of Lancaster

Canon John Hall (London), General Secretary of the Board of Education of the Church of England and of the National Society

Together with Revd Dr Charles Hill, European Secretary of the Council for Christian Unity.

The consultation concentrated on the following areas:

1. the relationship between Church and schools;
2. the training of teachers;
3. the education of children, families and adults in the parish;
4. the role of children and families in the worship of the parish.

The EKD delegates were impressed by the high level of involvement on the part of the Church of England in the area of Church schools, which they compared to the involvement of German Churches in the field of *diakonia*. The Diocese of Blackburn plays a particularly significant role in the field of education in the Church of England due to its high number of primary and secondary Church-aided schools.

Following their visits to schools and parishes, the members of the EKD delegation highlighted the following impressions:

- that the education of children, families and adults is based on a clear mission strategy and a unified concept of education;
- that conveying the significance of belonging to the Church has high priority;
- that in both churches and schools instruction regarding personal faith and spirituality is of particular importance;
- that students from different cultural and religious backgrounds are integrated in the Christian life of Church schools;
- that work in the area of education on the parish level is largely undertaken by volunteers;
- that participation of all ages in the worship life of the parish is the declared aim of educational work in the Church.

The EKD delegates were impressed by the fact that at St Martin's College, Lancaster, one of the most important higher education colleges run by the Church of England, teachers for all school subjects are trained with a clearly Christian agenda. Following on from this consultation, a link between St Martin's College of Higher Education, Lancaster, and the Evangelische Fachhochschule, Freiburg, was established.

As a result of the consultation it was pointed out that – particularly within already existing links between Landeskirchen and Kirchenkreisen and the Church of England – contacts between Protestant schools in Germany and Church of England schools are to be encouraged and developed. In addition, mutual visits of teachers of religious education and the sharing of in-service training opportunities are to be made possible.

The participants agreed that the EKD and the Church of England should work together with regard to the anti-discrimination legislation of the EU to maintain their right to continue to employ mainly Christian workers in Church institutions of education and *diakonia*.

delegation visit to the Rhineland, April 2001

Following on from the visit to Blackburn, the Evangelical Church in Germany hosted a delegation from the Church of England for five days of intensive consultation on the same theme of passing on the faith to the next generation. The consultation was based at the Pädagogisches-Theologisches Institut in Bonn-Bad Godesberg in the Rhineland, and the programme included a visit to Cologne and a joint service in the Old Catholic Church in Bonn where Bishop Joachim Vobbe presided and the Bishop of Coventry preached.

The delegations included Church leaders, Synod members and specialists in the field of youth work:

For the Church of England:

> The Rt Revd Colin Bennetts, Bishop of Coventry
>
> The Rt Revd Michael Bourke, Bishop of Wolverhampton and Co-Chairman of the Meissen Commission
>
> Mr Peter Ball, National Youth Officer, Board of Education
>
> Canon Peter Ballard, Diocesan Director of Education, Blackburn, member of the General Synod
>
> Mrs Anne Foreman, member of the General Synod and the Diocesan Board of Education, Guildford
>
> The Revd Richenda Leigh, Diocesan Youth Officer, Stepney, Diocese of London
>
> Ms Martha Middlemiss, Coordinator of the Young Adult Network, the General Synod
>
> Mrs Samantha Richards, Director of Studies, Degree Course in Youth Work, Oxford Brookes University
>
> Together with Revd Dr Charles Hill, European Secretary, Council for Christian Unity.

For the EKD:

> Bishop Dr h.c.Rolf Koppe, EKD Central Office, Hannover
>
> Bishop Dr Hans-Christian Knuth, Bishop for Schleswig, Co-Chairman of the Meissen Commission
>
> OKR Harald Bewersdorf, Düsseldorf, Head of the Education Department in the Evangelical Church in the Rhineland and member of the EKD Synod
>
> OKR Dr Jürgen Frank, Hannover, Head of the Education Department, EKD Central Office
>
> Oberbürgermeisterin Barbara Rinke, Nordhausen, member of the Presidium of the EKD Synod
>
> Herr Ottokar Schulz, Hannover, Head of the Ecumenical Department of the Arbeitsgemeinschaft der Evangelischen Jugend
>
> Frau Iris Wallat, Gössnitz, district youth officer and member of the EKD Synod
>
> Together with OKR Paul Oppenheim, Hannover, Co-Secretary of the Meissen Commission.

The participants visited local churches, confirmation classes and youth clubs, and considered issues such as process evangelism. They were impressed by creative experiments in using the electronic media to create new forms of community in which young people can explore Christian spirituality and engage with questions of faith.

Both our Churches regard passing on the faith to the next generation of young people and adults as vital for the ethical and cultural well-being of our societies. In this connection the English delegation was particularly impressed by the enduring significance of confirmation in the EKD Churches, and the high proportion of young Germans who attend the two-year confirmation course. This is admittedly different in the former East Germany.

A key issue is the relationship of confirmation preparation (and courses for adult enquirers) to the worshipping life of the congregation. The relationship of confirmation to admission to Holy Communion is also being discussed in both our Churches. Both the Church of England and the EKD Churches are mobilizing large numbers of volunteers in catechetical work. At the same time, however, there are significant constraints on what local congregations can achieve because of changing patterns of work and leisure at weekends.

Following this visit to the Rhineland, the Meissen Commission is making a number of significant recommendations to our two Churches. These envisage major discussions on the development of confirmation preparation, both nationally and in the context of local partnerships; promoting youth exchanges; and strengthening our cooperation in youth work at the national level. Those recommendations are set out fully in Sections 5.1–5.4 on pages 29–31.

synods

EKD synods

A member of the Meissen English committee has been present at each Synod of the EKD, which meets annually. The Revd Dr John Kelly, the Venerable Colin Williams, the Revd Martin Reakes-Williams and Mrs Tonie Smith attended the Synods held in Wetzlar, Münster, Leipzig and Braunschweig respectively. Each Synod takes a new theme for its main papers and in-depth debate. In 1997 the theme was Worship, in 1998 Europe, in 1999 Mission and Evangelism. The theme in 2000 was ecumenical, 'Eins in Christus' ('One in Christ'), and the Synod was addressed by Dr Konrad Raiser of the World Council of Churches, among others.

It is felt important to continue this tradition with its subsequent reporting back to the English committee. Many contacts have been made, and much has been learned in this way about current concerns and methods of working in the EKD member Churches.

General Synod of the Church of England

York, 1998

On behalf of the Meissen Commission, Frau Ursula Köhler represented the EKD at the General Synod of the Church of England held in York from 2 to 7 July 1998. She found it extremely helpful that Dr Colin Podmore of the Council for Christian Unity, the then Co-Secretary of the Meissen Commission, had prepared the visit so thoroughly and supplied the ecumenical guests with basic information about General Synod and interesting details about that particular group of sessions.

With the three houses of General Synod having to decide on their own dissolution – so that the Archbishops' Council could be established – the first meetings were of special interest. The guest was particularly impressed by the disciplined way in which the debate was carried on.

The close relations between the Church of England and the EKD were reflected in the great interest numerous members of Synod took in the Meissen process and in the German Protestant Churches.

York, 2000

The meeting of the General Synod of the Church of England held in York from 6 to 11 July 2000 was attended, on behalf of the Meissen Commission, by Dr Christof Theilemann of the EKD.

The main themes of the Synod were: the practical implementation of the establishment of provincial episcopal visitors following the acceptance of the ordination of women by the Church of England, and following on from that their possible representation in the House of Bishops; the theological evaluation of the possible consecration of women bishops; and an analysis of baptism practices and youth work in the Church.

As an observer, Dr Theilemann was impressed by the objective, fair and disciplined manner in which these sometimes controversial themes were discussed. He was also very grateful for the hospitality that was extended to him as an ecumenical guest through the Council for Christian Unity.

Following contacts made in York by Dr Theilemann, a very helpful and interesting visit was made by Church workers of the United Reformed Church to the EKD in Hannover.

the Evangelische Synode deutscher Sprache in Grossbritannien

The close relationships that already exist in many places between German Protestant churches in Great Britain and Anglican churches have deepened during this commission's period of office. The inclusion of the Synod in the relationship between the EKD and the Church of England has resulted in an increase in joint work. More and more 'Meissen services' are being celebrated alongside the now traditional Anglican–Protestant services, and this is raising public awareness of the Meissen Agreement.

It is especially in regions where both German and Anglican churches experience a high turnover – in university cities and in the London area – that the Meissen process is widely known.

In 1998, the first informal dialogue on ecclesiological issues was held between the Synod and the Church of England.

The Council for Christian Unity is regularly invited to Synod meetings, and for their part the Synod nominated Pfarrer Dr Uwe Vetter (London West) as a consultant member of the Meissen Commission.

In future there will be joint supervision of curates (Vikare/Vikarinnen) from EKD member Churches who are ministering with the Synod or in the Church of England, and they will be made familiar with the practical aspects of the Meissen Declaration.

the Anglican Diocese in Europe

In the last five years there has been further progress in enabling Anglicans in Germany to speak with one voice. The Council of Anglican Episcopal Churches in Germany (CAECG) has now been established as a registered association in German law and become a member Church of the Arbeitsgemeinschaft Christlicher Kirchen (comparable to Churches Together in Britain and Ireland).

The Church of England chaplaincies are now all part of the Deanery of Germany and the Archdeaconry of Scandinavia and Germany. Previously, the German chaplaincies were divided between four different archdeaconries. Thus all chaplaincies involved in the Meissen and Porvoo processes have been brought together in a way that reflects these agreements and furthers ecumenical cooperation. In addition, the Church of England Deanery of Germany has been represented on the Meissen Commission by the chaplain in Leipzig.

Most chaplaincies report that globalization and the growth of English as a world language mean an increasing interest in English-language worship among expatriate business people, refugees, and students of many nationalities, as well as local Germans. Most chaplaincies now see themselves as catering not just for those whose mother tongue is English, and not only for those with an Anglican background. The common element is the desire for worship in the English language.

In Leipzig, an agreement has been drawn up under the Meissen Agreement between the Anglican Diocese in Europe and the Lutheran Church of Saxony to enable the Anglican chaplain to have a regular ministry in congregations of the Lutheran Church of Saxony.

2001 has been a year of change for both Anglican jurisdictions in Germany, with new bishops being appointed for the Convocation of American Episcopal Churches in Europe and the Church of England Diocese in Europe. One of their tasks will be to take forward discussions that have begun in the last few years on bringing together the four Anglican jurisdictions in continental Europe (Church of England, Episcopalian, Lusitanian and the Spanish Reformed Episcopal Church).

exchange of information and cooperation between the Church offices

Much of the consultation between the Churches that the Meissen Declaration envisaged occurs at staff level. The co-secretaries of the Meissen Commission are, respectively, the Secretary for North and West Europe in the Europe Department of Section III (Ecumenical Relations and Work Abroad) of the EKD Kirchenamt and the European Secretary of the Council for Christian Unity of the Archbishops' Council of the Church of England. The servicing of the commission and work on its behalf, which requires the co-secretaries to be in frequent contact, has been greatly assisted by the introduction of the Internet, allowing for rapid and detailed communication by email. Organizing the various consultations, conferences and commission meetings, as well as a number of other meetings and visits that result from the work of the Meissen Commission and the intensification of bilateral relations as a result of the Meissen Declaration, is similarly the responsibility of the co-secretaries. Close contact between the two Church offices is a key feature of the relationship that has grown out of the Meissen Agreement.

The co-secretaries inform each other of all important developments. All General Synod papers are sent to the German co-secretary, and all *EKD-Texte* and other important publications are sent to the Anglican co-secretary. The Church office of the United Evangelical–Lutheran Church of Germany, which brings together all the Lutheran Landeskirchen of the EKD, contributes to the exchange of information by sending to the Council for Christian Unity details of decisions of its General Synod and information about courses at its training centre. There is a regular exchange of Church news services and periodicals.

The co-secretaries have also put other parts of Church House and the EKD Kirchenamt into contact with each other. In addition there is regular contact between the European Department of the EKD and the Church of England Board for Social Responsibility about cooperation between the Churches at European level within the Conference of European Churches (CEC) and its Commission for Church and Society based in Brussels.

Parishes, clergy and lay people continue to approach the EKD Kirchenamt with enquiries about the Church of England, and the

Council for Christian Unity answers many enquiries about the EKD from Church of England parishes and dioceses. The Internet has greatly facilitated such communication. Documents, information about and links to partner Churches are available on the national web pages of the EKD and the Church of England (www.ekd.de; www.cofe.anglican.org.uk/ccu).

prison chaplaincies

In the past 15 years, the prison chaplaincy services within the EKD and the British prison chaplaincy service have developed a strong and stable partnership. The primary contact persons on a regular basis are the representative of the Council of the EKD for ministry in places of detention and the respective Assistant Chaplain General of Her Majesty's Prison Service Chaplaincy. Both are also members of the International Prison Chaplains' Association (IPCA). Any matters connected with international ecumenical relationships and prison chaplaincy are discussed by a working group convened by the EKD representative, which includes prison chaplaincy representatives from the Roman Catholic Church and the Salvation Army alongside chaplains of the EKD.

Different representatives of the partner Churches have been participating in prison chaplaincy conferences on a national level on an annual or biennial basis since 1997. In addition, a curate from Hesse had the opportunity for a placement of several months in a British prison in 1999.

In August 1998, the Assistant Chaplain General Revd Bob Payne paid a three-day visit to the EKD representative in Berlin in order to discuss the continuation and intensification of their partnership. Part of their consultation was also attended by Revd Dr Christof Theilemann (a member of the Meissen Commission). The Meissen Commission was informed about the results of the consultation by Dr Theilemann and by a report by Revd Bob Payne to the Bishop of Wolverhampton.

It was agreed:

- to increase the exchange of relevant literature;
- to intensify the efforts to establish links between different types of institution (e.g. young offenders' institutions, women's prisons, etc.);
- to encourage prison chaplains and students of theology to continue to take part in training courses and placements in the other country;

- to put more effort into the integration of prison chaplaincy into existing links between Landeskirchen and dioceses as part of the Meissen process.

In individual cases, first signs of success are already visible. However, we also have to point out that due to the cutbacks in the prison chaplaincy representative office of the EKD and the process of restructuring at the chaplaincy headquarters of HM Prison Service, the available capacity for these efforts is less than it was in 1998. In principle, however, the commitment to the link is being maintained and fostered.

the German Protestant Kirchentag

Over the past quinquennium three Kirchentage have taken place, attracting thousands of participants from all over the world: in Leipzig in 1997, with the theme 'Auf dem Weg der Gerechtigkeit ist Leben' ('On the road to justice is life'); in Stuttgart in 1999, with the theme 'Ihr seid das Salz der Erde' ('You are the salt of the earth'); and in Frankfurt am Main in 2001, with the theme 'Du stellst meine Füsse auf weiten Raum' ('You have set my feet in a broad place').

At each assembly the commission has been represented by one of its members, with Revd Peter Townley present at Leipzig and Frankfurt, the Venerable Colin Williams at Stuttgart and the Bishop of Wolverhampton at Frankfurt. Usually there has been a Meissen stall at the 'Markt der Möglichkeiten' ('Marketplace') with attractive displays and material drawn from various partnerships. These have helped to heighten people's awareness of the agreement and its multifaceted possibilities. A Meissen Eucharist is now a familiar point on the Kirchentag programme with wide involvement and good attendance.

At the 1997 Kirchentag in Leipzig members of various partnerships, especially some that are involved in the Nürnberg–Hereford link, prepared a Meissen Eucharist and a stall at the Marketplace. The bilingual Eucharist was presided over by the Bishop of Gibraltar in Europe, the Rt Revd John Hind, and Oberkirchenrat Franz Peschke from Nürnberg preached. Some members of the Meissen Commission were involved in the service, which was a good opportunity for many English-speaking visitors to meet and to get in touch with people from Germany who are involved or interested in German–English partnerships. The stall at the Marketplace, which illustrated the deanery link between Schwabach (Kirchenkreis

Nürnberg) and Pontesbury (Diocese of Hereford), turned out to be a 'communication corner' and a meeting point for English guests.

While the Meissen Commission was not directly involved in the preparation of a Meissen service at the Kirchentag in Stuttgart in 1999, it played a leading role in bringing together representatives of partnerships from various EKD Churches and English dioceses at the Marketplace, and in preparing a Meissen Eucharist at the 2001 Kirchentag in Frankfurt am Main.

The host church for the Meissen service in Frankfurt was the Anglican Episcopal church of Christ the King, whose minister, the Revd Allan Sandlin, and parishioners were very welcoming. The service was presided over by the Episcopal Bishop for Europe, Jeffrey Rowthorne from Paris, and sung by the excellent parish choir. The Co-Chairman of the Meissen Commission and Bishop of Wolverhampton the Rt Revd Michael Bourke preached in German. Other assistants were the Old Catholic bishop the Rt Revd Joachim Vobbe, members of the Meissen Commission and the German Community of the Cross of Nails. The involvement of representatives from EKD Churches, the Church of England, the hosting American Episcopal Church and the Old Catholic Church helped the bilingual service to radiate a sense of ecumenical variety. The collection was dedicated to the ministry of reconciliation of Coventry Cathedral.

The smooth running of the wheels of the ecumenical movement is oiled by personal contact and friendship. Sharing in Bible studies and other activities including meeting at the International Centre has helped widen the ecumenical network.

'Church of England–EKD, for example Hereford–Nürnberg' was the title of a stall that had been prepared by a member of the Meissen Commission, Ursula Köhler, and another member of the partnership committee in Nürnberg. Apart from general information about the Church of England, the EKD and the Meissen Agreement, details about the partnership were shown. It was especially encouraging that a number of other links supported the stall in Frankfurt both through material about their work and through personal assistance. Thus the visitors were informed about the partnerships between Worcester and Magdeburg, Blackburn and Braunschweig (via a freshly produced CD-ROM), and Ely and Northelbe. During opening hours representatives of these and other partnerships, German and English members of the Meissen Commission and representatives of the American Episcopal community in Frankfurt were on hand to assist anyone interested.

With such a variety of people present, many interesting contacts were made and conversations carried on.

The commission believes that its involvement in the Kirchentag has made a significant contribution to wider awareness of the Meissen Agreement and to arousing interest for this work. Those already involved in partnerships appreciated the opportunity of exchanging thoughts and experience.

prayer letters

The commission has continued to send out letters to Anglican and German Protestant religious communities, requesting intercession for the work of the commission and for the unity of our Churches.

Eight of these prayer letters were sent out, in July 1996, spring and autumn 1997, summer 1998, spring and autumn 1999 and autumn 2000 and 2001. They listed topics of current concern, both secular and church-related, and gave brief information about the activities and progress of the commission's work.

These have been well received, and as a result Revd Peter Townley was asked to be a guest speaker at an international consultation of religious superiors at Mirfield after Easter 2000.

We very much value the prayerful support of our brothers and sisters throughout our two countries.

contributions to Anglo–German reconciliation

The growing unity between our Churches is part of, and contributes to, the growing reconciliation of our countries in the European context. We regard this as an important aspect of our responsibilities, and in the last few years it has been expressed in:

the Dresden Trust

For the past seven years a member of the Meissen Commission has represented the commission as a trustee of the Dresden Trust. This charitable organization has been raising money towards the rebuilding of the Protestant Frauenkirche, which was destroyed by the bombing of Dresden in 1945. At the request of the people of Dresden, the trust appealed for donations and held fund-raising concerts, dinners, exhibitions and numerous other events in order to finance the construction of the orb and cross which will be placed above the dome of the church when the building is completed in 2004.

In February 2000, the orb and cross were presented at impressive ceremonies in Dresden. Made by the firm of Grant Macdonald in London, and constructed as an exact copy of the original, the cross was presented by HRH the Duke of Kent as a gift from the British people as a lasting memorial to the victims of aerial bombardment everywhere, and as a symbol of reconciliation and renewal.

£600,000 has been raised so far, and fund-raising will continue in order to support the important spiritual significance and the 'human, scholarly and artistic activities' that are planned for the ecumenical role of the Frauenkirche in the future. Many personal contacts have been established during the period of the trust's involvement, and the project itself has done much to further goodwill, understanding and reconciliation between Britain and Dresden following the destruction of that city and the restrictions of the communist regime.

the Westminster Abbey statues

In July 1998, new stone figures representing notable Christian martyrs of the twentieth century were placed in empty niches at the west portal of Westminster Abbey. Among them was one notable figure who represented opposition within the German churches to Nazi oppression, Dietrich Bonhoeffer. As a sign of the Meissen relationship between the Church of England and the EKD, Präses Manfred Kock, Chairman of the EKD Council, attended the service of dedication of the new statues.

Following this service, Präses Kock met with the Archbishop of Canterbury at Lambeth Palace.

chapter 2

recommendations

The Meissen Commission makes the following recommendations to our Churches (many of which are included in the main text of the report):

1. the Meissen Commission

1.1 A new Meissen Commission should be appointed, with a term of office finishing on 31 December 2006. It should have five members on each side, including a bishop (or equivalent) as chairman and at least one clergy and one lay member. Two of the German members should come from the new Bundesländer.

1.2 Our Churches should request their sister Churches to appoint observers as follows:

(a) the Church in Wales, the Scottish Episcopal Church and the Church of Ireland to appoint one joint observer;

(b) the Council of the Anglican Episcopal Churches in Germany to nominate one observer for appointment by the Bishop of Gibraltar in Europe;

(c) the Evangelische Synode deutscher Sprache in Grossbritannien to appoint one observer.

1.3 The Meissen Commission should meet with the Porvoo Contact Group during the next five-year period.

2. theological conferences

2.1 Papers from the Springe and Cheltenham conferences should be published as soon as possible.

2.2 The Church of England should make an official response to the Leuenberg Agreement and the document *The Church of Jesus Christ*.

2.3 The Church of England should develop further its theological understanding of full visible unity as entailing the acceptance of the historic episcopate.

2.4 The Meissen Commission should then consider how the outcome of the above recommendations should be received in our Churches.

2.5 During the next five years, further theological conferences should be held to address the issues arising from the Cheltenham conference.

3. Local Ecumenical Partnerships (LEPs)

3.1 The EKD and its member Churches should familiarize themselves with the Local Ecumenical Partnership (LEP) model of partnerships between parishes and sector ministries.

3.2 The Meissen Commission should encourage the establishment of some pilot LEPs, including ministerial exchanges, under the provisions of Canon B 44 and German equivalents. The commission should evaluate these projects carefully and amend the guidelines if necessary.

3.3 The co-secretaries of the commission should serve as LEP advisers to encourage and train those involved in sponsoring bodies and local partnership groups.

3.4 Provided the initial pilot phase is successful, the Meissen Commission should encourage the formation of Local Ecumenical Partnerships between our churches.

3.5 The Meissen Commission should encourage the participation of theological teachers and students in LEPs to provide theological reflection.

4. delegation visits

4.1 Within the next five years there should be one visit by the Chairman of the Council of the EKD and other German Church leaders to England, and one visit by an archbishop and other Church of England leaders to Germany. These delegation visits should focus on issues of current concern to both Churches, as well as guiding the development of the Meissen relationship.

5. passing on the faith to the next generation

5.1 Our Churches should encourage exchanges involving schools (especially Church schools) and teachers of religious education.

5.2 The Meissen Commission should encourage dioceses and their German partner churches to:

(i) promote youth exchanges as a specific contribution to international understanding and reconciliation, exploring different forms of worship, space, story and spectacle for young people;

(ii) promote the sharing of information and practice in the recruitment, training and support of youth workers, paid and voluntary;

(iii) promote joint conferences on confirmation and evangelism which might include questions such as the following:

- What is the content and length of confirmation programmes offered by each partner and why?
- How do confirmation programmes relate to the worshipping community?
- What are the expected outcomes?
- What follow-up takes place after completion of confirmation programmes?
- What does each partner see as the purpose of confirmation?
- What is the relationship between teenage confirmation and the preparation of adult enquirers?

5.3 The Meissen Commission should invite the National Youth Office of the Church of England, through its Board of Education, and the Arbeitsgemeinschaft Evangelischer Jugend (AEJ) to develop existing and new links in order to:

(i) establish formal links between the young adult network of the Church of England and the assemblies of the AEJ;

(ii) encourage more English participation in the 2003 Kirchentag, and be directly represented on the British Kirchentag Committee;

(iii) establish a comparative research programme into the process of confirmation in each of the partner countries, reflecting particularly on the retention of young people within the Church;

(iv) explore possible connections with work in this field in the context of other international Church relationships;

(v) encourage exchanges for those working in the related academic field (e.g. trainers of teachers and leaders of confirmation preparation).

5.4 The Meissen Commission should invite the House of Bishops of the Church of England to consider the nature of confirmation preparation and the ways in which it is monitored and evaluated in the dioceses.

6. study exchanges

6.1 We recommend that English theological colleges and the Ministry Division of the Archbishops' Council explore new ways of enabling English students to draw on the strengths of theology in Germany.

6.2 The in-service training officers of our Churches should encourage periods of study in each other's countries in curacies, sabbaticals, etc.

6.3 The Meissen Commission should arrange meetings in each country for those who have undertaken an exchange, placement or extended period of study in the other country as part of their training for ministry to share and reflect on their experience.

7. libraries

7.1 The Meissen Commission should explore the future development of the Meissen Library in Durham, including possible sources of funding, and publicize the library widely.

8. prison chaplaincies

8.1 The Meissen Commission expresses the hope that the EKD will retain the capacity to support and develop international cooperation in its prison chaplaincy service.

9. prayer letters

9.1 The Meissen Commission recommends that prayer letters should continue to be distributed in both countries.

On behalf of the Meissen Commission:

The Rt Revd Hans-Christian Knuth, Bishop for Schleswig
The Rt Revd Michael Bourke, Bishop of Wolverhampton
Co-Chairmen of the Commission

London, 17 September 2001

appendix A
the Meissen Declaration*

'We the Church of England, the Federation of the Evangelical Churches in the German Democratic Republic with its member churches and the Evangelical Church in Germany with its member churches, on the basis of our sharing the common apostolic faith and in the light of what we have re-discovered of our common history and heritage, expressed in chapters I – V of *The Meissen Common Statement*, commit ourselves to strive together for full, visible unity.'

A (i) We acknowledge one another's churches as churches belonging to the One, Holy, Catholic and Apostolic Church of Jesus Christ and truly participating in the apostolic mission of the whole people of God;

(ii) we acknowledge that in our churches the Word of God is authentically preached and the sacraments of baptism and eucharist are duly administered;

(iii) we acknowledge one another's ordained ministries as given by God and instruments of his grace, and look forward to the time when the reconciliation of our churches makes possible the full interchangeability of ministers;

(iv) we acknowledge that personal and collegial oversight (*episkope*) is embodied and exercised in our churches in a variety of forms, episcopal and non-episcopal, as a visible sign of the Church's unity and continuity in apostolic life, mission and ministry.

B We commit ourselves to share a common life and mission. We will take all possible steps to closer fellowship in as many areas of Christian life and witness as possible, so that all our members together may advance on the way to full, visible unity.

---

* From *The Meissen Agreement: Texts*, CCU Occasional Paper No. 2, 1992.

As the next steps we agree:

(i) to continue official theological conversations between our churches, to encourage the reception of the theological consensus and convergence already achieved and to work to resolve the outstanding differences between us;*

(ii) to establish forms of joint oversight so that our churches may regularly consult one another on significant matters of faith and order, life and work;*

(iii) to participate in one another's worship, including baptism, eucharist and ordinations;

(iv) that authorized ministers of our churches may, subject to the regulations of the churches and within the limits of their competence, carry out the tasks of their own office in congregations of the other churches when requested;

> If these functions are to be exercised for an extended period of service rather than on a single occasion, an invitation from the appropriate authority is necessary for the carrying out of these tasks.

(v) that the Church of England invites members of the member churches of the Federation of the Evangelical Churches in the German Democratic Republic and the member churches of the Evangelical Church in Germany to receive Holy Communion according to the order of the Church of England; the member churches of the Federation of the Evangelical Churches in the German Democratic Republic and the member churches of the Evangelical Church in Germany invite members of the Church of England to receive Holy Communion according to their respective orders. We encourage the members of our churches to accept the eucharistic hospitality extended to them and thus express their unity with one another in the One Body of Christ;

(vi) that whenever in our churches the people of God assemble for eucharistic worship, the ordained ministers of our churches, in accordance with their rules, may share in the celebration of the eucharist in a way which advances beyond mutual eucharistic hospitality but which falls short of the full interchangeability of ministers.** Such eucharistic fellowship will reflect the presence

---

* Such steps will need to be agreed separately between the Church of England and the Federation of the Evangelical Churches in the GDR and between the Church of England and the Evangelical Church in Germany.

** Concelebration, in the sense of co-consecration, by word or gesture is not envisaged.

of two or more churches expressing their unity in faith and baptism, and demonstrate that we are still striving towards making more visible the unity of the One, Holy, Catholic and Apostolic Church and that we are strengthening and encouraging one another on the way to that goal in this eucharistic fellowship with the One Lord Jesus Christ;

Such services of the eucharist are presided over by an ordained minister. Only this person may say the eucharistic prayer.

In the eucharistic prayer the narrative of the institution is bound up with thanksgiving to the Father, the remembrance of the salvific work of Christ (*Anamnesis*) and the invocation of the Holy Spirit (*Epiklesis*).

In such services the rite used should be one authorized by the church of the presiding minister.

The liturgical arrangements, including the allotting of the different parts of the service, should be determined according to local circumstances and traditions.

An appropriate procedure for the elements remaining after the celebration must be followed. Each church should respect the practices and piety of the others. The best way of showing respect for the elements served in the eucharistic celebration is by their consumption, without excluding their use for communion of the sick.

Ministers should be vested in the manner appropriate to their tradition.

(vii) that whenever a bishop or minister accepts an invitation to take part in an ordination of another church this expresses the commitment of our churches to the unity and apostolicity of the Church. Until we have a reconciled, common ministry such participation in ordination cannot involve acts which by word or gesture might imply that this has already been achieved.

For the Church of England this means that a participating bishop or priest may not by the laying on of hands or otherwise do any act which is a sign of the conferring of Holy Orders. He may take part in a separate laying on of hands as an act of blessing.

appendix B
the Implementation Agreement*

the implementation by the Church of England and the Evangelische Kirche in Deutschland of the steps agreed in the Meissen Declaration

In the joint Declaration recommended in the Meissen Common Statement (the Meissen Declaration) the Church of England and the Evangelische Kirche in Deutschland and its member churches (hereinafter called 'the participating churches') have committed themselves 'to share a common life and mission' and to 'take all possible steps to closer fellowship in as many areas of Christian life and witness as possible, so that all our members together may advance on the way to full, visible unity' (Meissen, B). The participating churches now agree further practical steps towards that goal.

Partnerships

1. The participating churches shall encourage parishes, groups of parishes, deaneries, dioceses, cathedral churches and non-parochial church agencies and institutions to enter into partnerships with counterparts in each other's churches. Such partnerships shall involve visits and exchanges of lay people and ministers (whether in groups or as individuals), exchanges of information, shared worship, prayer and spiritual reflection, and joint discussions about matters of common concern. The Church of England and the Evangelische Kirche in Deutschland shall encourage dioceses and member churches to assist with funding and other resources for partnerships.

2. Where local partnerships exist between either of the participating churches and another church in Germany or England, the widening of such partnerships to include the Church of England or the Evangelische Kirche in Deutschland (as the case may be) is encouraged. Similarly, the involvement of other churches and Christians in partnerships covered by this agreement is encouraged.

---

* From *The Meissen Agreement: Texts*, CCU Occasional Paper No. 2, 1992.

Exchanges of ministers and church workers

3. The participating churches shall facilitate and encourage exchanges of ministers and other church workers, and find appropriate situations for those undertaking post-ordination training or in-service training.

4. Approval for exchanges and placements must be obtained in each case from the appropriate authority. In the case of the Evangelische Kirche in Deutschland this will be the Kirchenleitung of the member church concerned, and duties in public worship shall be performed in accordance with the liturgical rules of that member church. In the case of the Church of England this will necessarily involve the approval of the bishop of the diocese, and duties in public worship shall be performed in accordance with the Canons of the Church of England.

Theological colleges and students

5. The establishment of partnerships between individual colleges and courses of the Church of England and individual Protestant theological training institutes and colleges in Germany will be encouraged. Such partnerships may involve group visits, individual visits and hospitality, exchanges of students and lecturers, joint conferences and consultations about work and educational methods. The participating churches shall endeavour to assist their training institutions and colleges in obtaining funding for such partnerships.

6. The establishment of scholarships and schemes for a regular exchange of theological students, also open to university students, and students at church colleges and on courses which do not participate in a particular partnership, shall also be encouraged.

Libraries

7. The Church of England and the Evangelische Kirche in Deutschland shall help each other to establish a library of Anglican studies in Germany and a library of German Protestant studies in England. Although housed in particular colleges or institutions, the libraries will be regarded as a resource for the whole church.

Conferences

8. The Church of England, the Evangelische Kirche in Deutschland and the Bund der Evangelischen Kirchen shall maintain a series of official

conferences of theologians and experts in various aspects of the faith and order, life and work of the Church. These conferences shall encourage the reception of the theological consensus and convergence already achieved, and work to resolve the outstanding differences between the participating churches (Meissen, B (i)).

Towards joint oversight

9.   Once in the lifetime of each Council the Evangelische Kirche in Deutschland shall invite the General Synod of the Church of England to send a delegation to visit the Evangelische Kirche in Deutschland with its member churches. The delegation shall include at least one member each of the Houses of Bishops, Clergy and Laity of the General Synod. The delegation should include a member of the Standing Committee and, where possible, one of the Presidents of the General Synod. Once in the lifetime of each General Synod, the Church of England shall invite the Evangelische Kirche in Deutschland to send a delegation to visit the Church of England. The delegation shall include members of the Council, including, where possible, its Chairman or his deputy, and at least one each of the bishops, clergy and lay members of the Synod or Kirchenkonferenz of the Evangelische Kirche in Deutschland.

10.   The House of Bishops of the Church of England shall, at least once in each five year period, invite the council of the Evangelische Kirche in Deutschland to nominate a person with personal oversight in one of the member churches of the Evangelische Kirche in Deutschland to participate, with the right to speak but not to vote, in a residential meeting of the House of Bishops of the General Synod. The Evangelische Kirche in Deutschland shall, at least once in the lifetime of each Council, invite a bishop of the Church of England to participate, with the right to speak but not to vote, in a meeting of the Kirchenkonferenz of the Evangelische Kirche in Deutschland (Meissen, B (ii)).

Evangelische Synode Deutscher Sprache in Grossbritannien; Diocese in Europe

11.   Co-operation in all areas of church life and work between the Church of England and the Evangelische Synode Deutscher Sprache in Grossbritannien as well as between the Evangelische Kirche in Deutschland and the Diocese in Europe shall be encouraged.

Instruments for joint action

12. In order to co-operate in fulfilling their common mission, the Church of England and the Evangelische Kirche in Deutschland may jointly and also together with other churches establish agencies or offices, organize commissions, committees or special ministries, or undertake other such activities. Unless agreed otherwise, such joint activities shall operate under the authority of the Sponsoring Body.

13. The terms of reference shall be agreed separately in each case. Unless otherwise agreed, the expenses of such joint activities shall be shared on an equal basis.

The Sponsoring Body

14. With effect from 1 March 1991, the Church of England and the Evangelische Kirche in Deutschland shall establish a Sponsoring Body. Its responsibility shall be to oversee the implementation of the Meissen Declaration and the practical steps set out above, and to encourage the participating churches to take all possible steps to closer fellowship on the way to full, visible unity.

15. It shall consist of the following members:

a bishop of the Church of England as co-chairman,

a clergy member of the Church of England,

a lay member of the Church of England

(all appointed for a period of five years by the Archbishops of Canterbury and York on the recommendation of the Council for Christian Unity of the General Synod);

a bishop or equivalent minister of the Evangelische Kirche in Deutschland as co-chairman,

a clergy member of the Evangelische Kirche in Deutschland,

a lay member of the Evangelische Kirche in Deutschland

(all appointed by the Council of the Evangelische Kirche in Deutschland for a period of five years).

16. A member of staff of the Council for Christian Unity of the General Synod and a member of staff of the European Department of the Kirchenamt of the Evangelische Kirche in Deutschland shall act as joint secretaries of the Sponsoring Body.

17. The Sponsoring Body shall meet at least once a year, alternately at the invitation of the Church of England and of the Evangelische Kirche in Deutschland. Normally each church shall pay the travel expenses of its own delegates, while all other expenses shall be borne by the host church.

18. The duties of the Sponsoring Body shall include the following:

(a)   To give guidelines and recommendations with regard to the implementation of the steps agreed in B(i)-(vii) of the Meissen Declaration and to co-ordinate practices of the dioceses of the Church of England and the member churches of the Evangelische Kirche in Deutschland.

(b)   Mutual consultation and exchange on questions of faith and order, life and work, whenever they arise.

(c)   To remind the participating churches of their ecumenical responsibilities when they propose to take steps which might affect their partner church.

(d)   To ensure that an extensive and regular exchange of information between the participating churches occurs.

(e)   To define themes and subjects for joint consideration by the participating churches, at consultations and conferences held under this agreement.

19. Towards the end of each five year period, the Sponsoring Body shall review the progress the participating Churches have made during that period on the way to visible unity, and their fulfilment of the pledges they have made. At the same time, it shall review this paper, suggesting any alterations or additions which might seem desirable.

20. The English and German texts of this agreement are equally authentic.

Berlin, 2 February 1991

For the Church of England:

Philip Mawer

The Secretary-General of the General Synod

appendix C

topics covered in commission meetings

In addition to exchanging information and dealing with its main agenda, the commission considered the following main subjects in depth:

- international ecumenical events and reconciliation
- the Concordat of Agreement in the United States
- the joint Lutheran–Roman Catholic Declaration on the Doctrine of Justification
- relations with the Old Catholic Church
- prison chaplaincy
- developments in the Convocation of American Episcopal Churches in Germany
- the Reuilly Common Statement
- stewardship
- the Network of City Centre Churches
- the diaconate
- the situation in Ireland
- the Stephen Lawrence Inquiry
- problems of rural ministry
- the practical consequences of the Porvoo Agreement
- Anglican–Lutheran cooperation in Africa.

At each meeting there has been an agenda item (*Berichte zur Lage*) under which the commission has discussed current issues of concern to our Churches. These have included:

- the debate concerning religious instruction in Brandenburg
- the UK general election
- the General Synod debate on the House of Bishops report *Issues in Human Sexuality*
- changing moods in eastern Germany
- the EKD in the context of European ecumenism
- the Lambeth Conference 1998
- the Jubilee Year 2000
- the creation and work of the Archbishops' Council

- the background to devolution in Scotland
- consultations on the role of bishops in the Second Chamber of Parliament (House of Lords)
- Expo 2000 in Hannover
- youth and radicalism in eastern Germany
- millennium events
- *Common Worship*
- asylum seekers and immigrants
- genetically modified food
- the foot and mouth disease crisis
- Church schools.

appendix D

Anglo-German diocesan links

Baden	
Freiburg	Guildford
Lörrach	Canterbury
Bavaria	Bristol
Bayreuth	Chichester
Nürnberg	Hereford
Berlin-Brandenburg	London
Braunschweig	Blackburn
Bremen	Worcester
Hannover	
Hildesheim	Chelmsford
Hannover	Bristol
Osnabrück	Derby
Hessen & Nassau	
Frankfurt	Birmingham
Mecklenburg	Lichfield
Nordelbien	Ely
Rhineland	Durham
Bonn	Oxford
Dortmund	Greater Manchester
Düsseldorf	Oxford (Reading)
Koblenz	Norwich
Köln	Liverpool
Saxony	
Chemnitz I/II	London Willesden
Chemnitz I	Manchester
Dresden	Coventry
Erfurt	Bradford
Leipzig	Stretford
	Milton Keynes
Magdeburg	Worcester
Westfalen	
Bielefeld	London (Pinner)
Hattingen-Witten	Sheffield
Lünen	Manchester/Salford

report of the third Meissen theological conference, Springe, 10–15 March 1999

the third theological conference held under the Meissen Agreement

'The Unity We Seek'/'Die Einheit, die wir anstreben'

Conference Report

Introduction

This third Meissen theological conference took as its theme 'The Unity We Seek', thereby continuing the work of the second conference on 'Visible Unity and the Ministry of Oversight'. The subject matter of the various papers followed this theme closely, as can be seen from the following record. More importantly, the conference was also governed by the provisions of the 1991 Meissen Declaration, and therefore the agreement in faith reached by the Evangelical Church in Germany and the Church of England.

As acknowledged in the 1991 Declaration, there is a remaining difference between our two churches over episcopal succession, and the following papers and conference common statement deal with that difference quite explicitly. It is very important, however, to see our discussion of this difference within the greater framework of communion, fellowship, prayer and love that was recognised in the Meissen Declaration, and that has been nurtured by much work since then. In undertaking the work of this conference, delegates had in mind the conviction that both churches are further down the road towards full visible unity, and that both churches are working together towards the realisation of this goal.

List of papers

There follows a record of the conference papers, listed in the order in which they were delivered:

1. Alan Falconer   'The unity we seek – the wider ecumenical context'

2. Thomas Seville   'Biblical introduction: unity in the New Testament'

3. Mark Chapman   'The politics of episcopacy'

4. Wilhelm Hüffmeier   'Einheit in unseren Kirchen – Theorie und Praxis, Erfahrungen und Hindernisse'

5. Peter Kevern   'Hearing the voice of the particular in ecumenical discourse'

6. Eilert Herms   'Thesen: Warum suchen wir die Einheit? Sozialethische Argumente'

7. Andreas Lindemann   'Biblische Einführung: Sichtbare Einheit im Neuen Testament'

8. Tord Harlin   'How is unity made visible? The Porvoo conversations'

9. Christopher Hill   'Visible unity within the Anglican Communion: What role do bishops have in making unity visible?'

10. Dorothea Wendebourg   'Sichtbare Einheit in der Evangelischen Kirche in Deutschland'

11. Gareth Jones   'Visibility as ecclesiological criterion'

12. Rowan Williams   'The goal of full unity — the gospel of the kingdom'

13. Juhani Forsberg   'The goal of full unity from a Lutheran perspective'

14. Paul Avis   'Achieving unity by stages'

Statement:

We agree that we participate fully in the unity of the Church of Jesus Christ. This unity is visibly (*wahrnehmbar*) given in the proclamation of the Word and the administration of the Sacraments, through which Christ unites the faithful with himself and each other.

We agree that the structures are always related to this given unity. We discussed how this applies to particular structures.

We agree that a common life based on this unity leads to common witness, common service and the formation of the various structures required for their realisation, which evolve in particular contexts.

In this context, the striving for 'full visible unity' is not understood as an attempt to add something to the visible unity that Christ has already given in Word and Sacraments, but rather as the endeavour by our churches to witness to this unity and respond more faithfully to what it promises, more comprehensively.

This witness equally serves the particularity and the universality, as well as the diversity and the unity, of the common life of the Body of Christ.

Arising from our discussion of the papers listed above we identified the following important themes for further study:

- the relationship between common priesthood and the ordained ministry;
- the possibility of a theology of gift, with special reference to ministry and episcopacy;
- the relationship between the historic episcopate and the threefold ministry;
- the relationship between the historic episcopate and historical episcope;
- linguistic and conceptual problems arising from the use of

    visibility/discernibility

    reconciliation/recognition/acknowledgement

    sign/witness

- the relevance of the doctrine of justification for the doctrine of the Church and its ministry;
- possible difficulties arising from parallel ecclesial jurisdictions;
- the relationship between the common statement on full visible unity, made above, and paragraph 16 of the Meissen Agreement.

Recommendations to the Meissen Commission:

We recommend that there be a further theological conference, if possible of the same composition, to undertake further work on these stated themes. We propose that such a conference take place during the periods 14–19 March or 21–26 March 2001.

Springe, 15 March 1999

appendix F

report of the fourth Meissen theological conference, Cheltenham, 14–19 March 2001

'Ten Years On – Ways Forward from Meissen'

1. The fourth Meissen Theological Conference took as its theme 'Ways Forward from Meissen', continuing the work of the third conference on 'The Unity We Seek'.

   The first task of the conference was to describe the current theological issues of the Meissen relationship against the wider ecumenical context. Reference was made to the various commitments and dialogues of the EKD, the British and Irish Anglicans, and of Lutherans, Reformed and Anglicans worldwide, including the Episcopal–Lutheran Agreement in the USA. For the partners represented at the Conference, the most recent fruit of this work was the Reuilly Common Statement, inspired by the Meissen process and to be signed in summer 2001 by the Anglican Churches of the British Isles, and the French Lutheran and Reformed Churches.

   The ecclesiological text *The Church of Jesus Christ*, published by the Leuenberg Church Fellowship (1995), was considered from EKD, Anglican and wider ecumenical perspectives in relation to the Meissen process. Delegates undertook a similar task, focusing on the theme of *episkope*, with papers on the document *Bishops in Communion* published by the Church of England House of Bishops (2000).

   The frame of reference of these documents provided a structure for the discussion of ways forward in Meissen: in matters of unity, witness and mission.

   In the course of our conversations, the Anglican and German Protestant delegations came to appreciate each other's views more fully in the light of the experience as well as the ambiguity of our histories. In particular, the Anglicans learnt to recognize that the witness to the apostolic continuity of the gospel was possible in the German Reformation only through breaking with the episcopal structures of the time. For their part, the German delegates recognized the value of visible continuity in pastoral oversight as a sign of the apostolic continuity of the church.

It was recommended that the Church of England formally considers the Leuenberg study *The Church of Jesus Christ*.

2. This conference took as the basis of its work the common ground already established between our churches in the Meissen Declaration § 17. During the course of its discussions the conference again and again found itself reaffirming:

'(i) We acknowledge one another's churches as churches belonging to the One, Holy, Catholic and Apostolic Church of Jesus Christ and truly participating in the apostolic mission of the whole people of God;

(ii) we acknowledge that in our churches the Word of God is authentically preached and the sacraments of baptism and eucharist are duly administered;

(iii) we acknowledge one another's ordained ministries as given by God and instruments of his grace;

(iv) we acknowledge that personal and collegial oversight (*episkope*) is embodied and exercised in our churches in a variety of forms, episcopal and non-episcopal, as a visible sign of the Church's unity and continuity in apostolic life, mission and ministry.'

3. In our discussion of the Leuenberg study *The Church of Jesus Christ* we found ourselves in agreement with the following fundamental points:

- Both the Meissen Agreement and the Leuenberg study state that everything that is said about the church, its foundation, its shape and its mission, must be seen in the context of the saving action of the triune God in history. This reality requires us to distinguish and relate God's activity and human activity in such a way that human activity must be understood as being a visible witness to God's action in constituting, maintaining and perfecting the church.

- The one foundation of the Church is the Lord Jesus Christ who makes himself present in the Church through the proclamation of the gospel and celebration of the sacraments in the power of the Spirit. It is this foundation that is served by the pastoral ministry given to the Church by God in Christ through the Holy Spirit.

- The life of the Church, grounded in this foundation and nurtured by this ministry, has taken different forms in history. While these forms have been shaped by contingent historical factors they cannot be arbitrary but must bear visible witness to the foundation of the Church in God's action as it is proclaimed by the word and celebrated in the sacraments.

- 'The Church has been called to be an instrument of God for the actualisation of God's universal will to salvation' (TCJC 3.2, p. 103). In order to fulfil this calling the Church must continually be conformed to its foundation in Christ. When it is faithful to its foundation and obedient to its calling the Church points away from itself and its structures to Christ.

4. In acknowledging 'one another's churches as churches belonging to the One, Holy, Catholic and Apostolic Church of Jesus Christ' (Meissen 17 A (i)) we see this one foundation as present in our churches in different shapes. In this we recognize God's providence at work in gathering his people from many contexts. We also confess that we often have failed to respond to God's will for his church. Our memories reflect both continuities and discontinuities in our respective histories. These memories have to be respected as manifesting God's ongoing engagement in our history. In this light we trust in God's promise to guide us on our way forward together.

5. In acknowledging that communal, collegial and personal oversight is exercised in our churches in a variety of forms (cf. Meissen 17 A (iv)) we recognize in these forms a visible witness to our churches' apostolic life, mission and ministry. Therefore it would not be right for one church to require the other to adopt its own ordering of the liturgy, the ministry, and the church government. We believe that § 16 of the Meissen Common Statement is to be read in the light of this principle. This also accords with §§ 37–40 of the Reuilly Agreement.

6. In each of our Churches we discern a number of common features which reflect the same underlying theological principles. These common features include: a common intention in ordaining ministers of Word and Sacrament in the Church of Jesus Christ, an ordered transmission of authority, a distribution of authority that is both dispersed and focussed, the office of personal oversight in its varying descriptions, the conferring of this office in a liturgical act including prayer with the laying on of hands. All our forms of exercising oversight are grounded in the ministry of word and sacrament and essentially are related to the royal priesthood of all baptized believers. In each other's ordering of this visible witness we recognize a common intention to remain faithful to the teaching and fellowship of the Church of the apostles. They all stand under the Word of God as witnessed in Scripture.

7. As a visible witness to the *koinonia* of the triune God with his people the Church is a sign and instrument of the Kingdom of God and in this way becomes a foretaste of the world to come. It bears witness to the unity, holiness, catholicity and apostolicity which are God's gift. This is why the gospel of Jesus Christ, the foundation of the Church, serves as the fundamental norm for its life. The structures of the church are there to enable the life of the church to be true to its foundation and serve its *koinonia* and mission through space and time. The *koinonia* which God gives informs the practice of ecclesial communion in all its dimensions: in the assembly of God's people under the Word of God, in the ministry of the Word and Sacrament and in the exercise of Church government.

8. In order to strengthen the bonds of communion between our Churches and to continue to realize the vision of our shared future we propose that we continue to work towards

   ● deeper theological agreement in our understanding of the ministry and ministries (e.g. the ministry in its relation to the royal priesthood of the baptized, the nature of the diaconate, and the issue of the 'threefold ministry');
   ● developing various forms of collegiality in the exercise of all forms of oversight (visitation, confirmation, ordination);
   ● considering the practice of confirmation within the communion of our churches;
   ● theological reflection on our churches' mission to our societies in the European context, including the theological foundations and criteria of our engagement with ethical problems;
   ● interchangeability of ministries in the context of our shared future.

Further progress in these areas would strengthen and make more explicit the communion that we already affirm and celebrate in the Meissen Agreement.

appendix G

model covenant and guide-lines on a constitution

for congregations of the Church of England and the Evangelische Kirche in Deutschland (EKD) in covenanted partnership under the Meissen Agreement

introduction

This is a model not a straitjacket. It outlines the main issues and areas to be considered in drafting a constitution for a new Local Ecumenical Partnership under the Meissen Agreement or for revising an existing one:

1. It is anticipated that an LEP under the Meissen Agreement would adopt the Covenant model currently used in a number of contexts. The model *Declaration of Intent or Covenant* and *Guidelines for a Constitution for Congregations in Covenanted Partnership*, published by the CTE Group for Local Unity in 1998, have been used as the basis for the draft Meissen LEP documents.

2. The basic assumption is that Meissen LEPs would arise from partnership or twinning arrangements and would probably be set up as a result of the following initial local interest:

   2.1 Two parishes/congregations within the existing framework of well-established diocesan/Landeskirche partnerships will consider the possibility of formalizing their partnership as an ecumenical covenant. There would have to be evidence of an enduring relationship. The idea of an LEP may originate from the parishes or may be suggested by the Meissen Commission or the Diocese/Landeskirche.

   2.2 The basic intent must include a clear commitment to joint mission (for example, evangelization and mission in the secular context of the parishes) and a commitment to regular visits during which the parishes will work together at their common goals. The contacts may include ministerial and lay exchanges and/or appointments.

3. The **Diocese and Landeskirche**, acting upon the expression of local interest, would need to

3.1   Set up for the proposed LEP a Sponsoring Body, which would include members exercising authority and oversight meeting within an agreed pattern.

3.2   Ensure that members of the Sponsoring Body are equipped with the necessary knowledge of the history and ecclesiology of the partner churches and of their appointments systems and structures, and with an awareness of their current concerns and priorities.

3.3   Be aware of how the activity of the Sponsoring Body fits in with other ecumenical commitments at the intermediate level in which the Diocese is involved, especially where the United Reformed and/or the Methodist Churches are a partner. These Churches are in full communion with the EKD through the Leuenberg Agreement.)

3.4   Determine how the Sponsoring Body would relate to home church structures, in particular accountability to synods and those exercising oversight.

4. The **Sponsoring Body** would

4.1   Draw up, in consultation with the parishes, a Declaration of Intent or Covenant and a Constitution for the Covenant partnership.

4.2   Make arrangements for the approval of the Constitution by the church authorities.

Note: For the CofE this would be the Diocesan Registrar, with the guidance of the Diocesan Ecumenical Officer.

4.3   Undertake to provide ongoing support and training and establish a system of review with appropriate questions to be asked.

5. The **Meissen Commission** would

5.1   Where appropriate, encourage and initiate local partnerships.

5.2   Provide guidelines on all aspects of the process (including a model Constitution) to Dioceses and Landeskirchen.

5.3   Arrange language courses, especially for English clergy preparing for service in Germany.

5.4   Appoint a specialist LEP Officer for each country.

5.5 Monitor the Sponsoring Bodies and receive LEP review reports.

5.6 Encourage ordinands and theologians to spend time in Meissen LEPs.

5.7 Liaise with the German Synod in England and with the Diocese in Europe to consider whether and how their congregations might become involved in Meissen LEPs.

6. These documents are designed mainly for partnerships between parishes, but the broad principles apply equally to LEPs arising in other contexts (for example: university, prison or industrial chaplaincies, Forces chaplaincies in Germany, the Diocese in Europe and the *Deutsche Evangelische Synode in Grossbritannien*). In these cases, other forms of constitution may be necessary, and advice should be sought from the Co-Secretaries of the Meissen Commission.

a model declaration of intent/covenant for congregations of the Church of England and the Evangelische Kirche in Deutschland (EKD) in covenanted partnership under the Meissen Agreement: local covenant between St John's, Praisetown, and Trinitas Gemeinde, Berlin-Lobedorf

In obedience to the call of Christ, we, the ministers and people of

ST JOHN'S PARISH CHURCH, PRAISETOWN (Church of England, Diocese of London), and

TRINITAS GEMEINDE, BERLIN-LOBEDORF (Evangelische Kirche in Berlin-Brandenburg),

who have increasingly shared our Christian life in a variety of ways over recent years, now feel a need to show our love for God and for one another by a more formal commitment to grow together in doing His will.

We confess our Faith in One God,
                    the Father, Creator,
                    the Son, Jesus Christ, our Lord and Saviour,
                    the Holy Spirit,
          guiding His Church, the Body of Christ, into all truth.

We recognize the Gospel of Christ to be authentically present in our two churches and in their ordinances of Word and Sacrament.

We repent of all that is sinful in our past histories and present attitudes.

We rejoice in the riches of the traditions we have inherited and seek to share them more fully with one another in the unity which is the will and gift of God.

We seek a deepening of our communion with Christ and with one another.

We covenant to seek to make our unity more visible, even though in our pilgrimage together we cannot foresee the form it will eventually take.

We therefore make this commitment to God and to each other.

We commit ourselves and our churches

a) To move through co-operation to clear commitment to each other, to make more visible the unity which Christ gives to us and for which he prayed, and to join in common evangelism and service to the world.

b) To engage in joint worship, prayer and study so that we may know and value each other and seek God's will for His people.

c) To work together in pastoral, social and evangelistic outreach into our communities, to learn from each other's experience in mission, and to seek new ways of responding to the call to mission in our common European context.

d) To publicize and promote the life and worship of our churches by joint means wherever possible, and to share our experience and reflect theologically upon it with our sponsoring churches and with the Meissen Commission.

To achieve these commitments we will:

a) Develop a Local Partnership Group, including clergy and lay representatives of each church, to meet at least once a year for prayer, study, consultation, and a review of progress. This Local Partnership Group will be responsible for promoting the Partnership in our congregations and encouraging joint mission activity.

b) Explore the possibility of making ordained or lay appointments from the partner church within the guidelines of the attached Constitution. Such appointments would be made by the receiving church in full consultation with the Sponsoring Body and the

Local Partnership Group, and would be consonant with Confessional procedures.

SIGNED by the Parish Ministers and *** lay representatives of each church.

COUNTERSIGNED BY OFFICIAL DENOMINATIONAL REPRESENTATIVES SERVING ON THE Sponsoring Body, and by a representative of the Meissen Commission.

NOTE: *Original versions of the covenant in English and German should be signed during the course of a solemn act of worship (either in England or Germany or both) attended by as many people as possible from the partner churches, by at least one Sponsoring Body representative from each denomination represented, and by a representative of the Meissen Commission. It may be desirable to provide an opportunity for those attending to add their own signature to one large sheet. Copies should be made and displayed in the foyer or worship area of each church. The document can be copied and postcards made for individual use.*

guidelines for a constitution for congregations of the Church of England and the Evangelische Kirche in Deutschland (EKD) in covenanted partnership under the Meissen Agreement

1. Name
a) The Local Ecumenical Partnership shall be known as (specify).
b) The Partnership comprises (specify Church of England) parish in the (specify Deanery and Diocese), and (specify EKD) church within the (local church district) of (specify Landeskirche).

NOTE: *The name will aim to specify the localities as clearly as possible. The Partner Churches should be listed here or reference made to an appendix setting out the names of Partner Churches. Further denominational partners (eg: other English-speaking congregations, a German-speaking congregation in England or a congregation of the Diocese in Europe or the Old Catholic Church) should be included where they are involved in the Partnership.*

2. Area

a) The Ecumenical Partnership primarily serves the communities/ neighbourhoods of (specify) and those who associate with its churches and benefit from its ministry. (Add, if appropriate: For (name of the Church of England church in the Local Ecumenical Partnership) the area of ministry shall be (designate boundaries/ see map). For (name of the EKD church in the Local Ecumenical Partnership) the area of ministry shall be (designate boundaries/ see map).)

NOTE: *The cohesiveness of the localities will be a factor in the areas to be covered and thus which congregations will be partners. More than one Church of England parish may be involved – for example, in a united benefice. For the Church of England, see Ecumenical Relations Code of Practice 23.*

3. Sponsoring Body

a) The Partnership looks for support and oversight to its Sponsoring Body and will be accountable to the partner churches through the Sponsoring Body.

b) Any unresolved matters shall be referred to the Sponsoring Body for consideration.

c) The Sponsoring Body shall ensure that the Partnership and this Constitution are officially endorsed by the relevant bodies of the two Churches (Synod, Bishop's Council, Diocesan Pastoral Committee, etc.).

d) The members of the Sponsoring Body shall ensure that this Partnership is drawn to the attention of any other Sponsoring Body or Ecumenical Council in which the Diocese or Landeskirche is involved.

e) The Sponsoring Body shall consist of the Bishop of the Diocese of .... and the Bishop or Chairman of the Landeskirche .... or their representatives; the Ecumenical Officers of the Diocese and Landeskirche; an Oberkirchenrat, Archdeacon or Legal representative of each Church.

f) The Sponsoring Body shall receive the Annual Report from the Local Partnership Group (see 7(d) below), and shall meet at least once every seven years to review the LEP. It is desirable for the members of the Sponsoring Body to meet more regularly, especially where there is a change of personnel, to maintain the trust and friendship on which these partnerships depend.

g) The Sponsoring Body shall invite the LEP Officers appointed by the Meissen Commission to its meeting to maintain regular two-way contact between the Meissen Commission and the Sponsoring Body, and to provide advice, support and training for the Sponsoring Body.

h) The Sponsoring Body shall appoint its ecumenical officers to act as link persons with the churches of the Partnership, and to provide advice, support and training to them.

i) The Sponsoring Body shall establish a system of reviews and shall agree the questions which should be asked (see 9 below).

NOTE: *A review every seven years is required by Canon B44.2(i) of the Church of England as a condition for the re-designation of the LEP by the Bishop. CTE has produced a booklet,* Guidelines for the Review of Local Ecumenical Partnerships (1999)*, which will need adapting.*

4. Baptism and membership

a) Infant and Adult Baptism shall continue to be administered according to the rite and/or practice of the constituent denominations.

b) The legal requirements of each local church to keep a register of baptisms and confirmations/membership shall be met as appropriate.

c) Each Church's practice in preparing candidates and their families for Baptism, and the relationship between Adult Baptism and Confirmation, should be the subject of careful study, discussion and evaluation by the Local Partnership Group.

d) Where a German Pastor is working in an Anglican congregation, Confirmation shall be administered according to the use of the Church of England by an Anglican Bishop. Where an Anglican priest is working in a congregation of the EKD, Confirmation shall be administered according to the use of the Landeskirche by another Pastor of the Landeskirche.

e) If special circumstances make it desirable to hold occasional or regular Anglican/EKD services of Confirmation, the Meissen Commission shall provide guidelines for the Sponsoring Body about the rite, the ministers who should participate and the implications for those so confirmed in terms of membership.

NOTE: *The circumstances may include a Local Ecumenical Partnership between an EKD parish and a congregation of the Diocese in Europe, or between a CofE parish and a congregation of the Deutsche Evangelische Synode in Grossbritannien. For the Church of England see Canon B44.4(1)(e) and Ecumenical Relations Code of Practice 108 to 116.*

f) Membership discipline shall continue to be a matter for each Church/denomination following its own procedures.

5. Prayer, worship and the Eucharist

a) The Partnership shall respect the faith and practice of its member denominations in relation to prayer, worship and the Eucharist.

b) Regular prayer for the Partnership and for wider ecumenism shall be a feature of the ongoing life and worship of each of the partner churches. To that end, prayer materials shall be compiled and kept updated.

c) Whenever there is united worship (eg: during exchanges) it shall safeguard and express the doctrines, practices, traditions and developing traditions of each participating denomination and be conducted in accordance with denominational practices and/ or using ecumenical and bilingual rites approved by the Sponsoring Body.

d) Ordained priests, pastors or other duly authorized persons shall preside at the Eucharist as permitted by denominational legislation. In Anglican churches the provision of Eucharistic services at which a non-Anglican minister presides shall be in accordance with Canon B44.

NOTE: *For the Church of England see Canon B44.4(1)(d), (e) & (f), 4(2) and B44.5 and Ecumenical Relations Code of Practice 75 to 95. B44.4(1)(f)&9 explain that 'minister' in relation to any other participating church means any person ordained to the ministry of word and sacraments. This means that B44(1)(f) may not provide for probationer ministers, Vikare/Vikarinnen or authorized lay persons to preside at the Eucharist. Good and sensitive practice is to advertise the service as 'according to ...x... tradition'.*

e) The forms and frequency of Eucharistic worship should follow the regulations of the partner churches. Due regard should be paid to the Eucharistic theology and sensitivities of each tradition in the administration of Holy Communion and the disposal of remaining Eucharistic elements.

f) At any Eucharistic celebration it shall be made clear that any who for whatever reason are unable to receive communion are invited to come forward for a blessing.

NOTE: *For the Church of England, see Canon B15A(1).*

g) The churches of the Partnership should be encouraged to agree a policy in relation to children and Holy Communion, and this should be approved by the Sponsoring Body.

h) In arranging services encouragement shall be given to the participation of Lektore, Readers and others authorized as leaders of worship or as preachers.

NOTE: *For the Church of England, see Canon B44.4(1)(a) and (b).*

6. Ecumenical appointments

a) The Local Partnership Group shall consider, in consultation with the Sponsoring Body, whether there is scope EITHER for a ministerial exchange for a limited period OR for the appointment of a German pastor in the English parish or an Anglican priest in the German parish for a fixed period of years.

b) Such ministers would carry out the normal ministerial functions of word and sacrament, leadership and pastoral care, within the disciplines of the 'host' and the 'sending' churches.

NOTE: *For the Church of England the Bishop provides a written instrument according to the provisions of Canon B44.4(l). A draft is available from the Council for Christian Unity. (These provisions mean, among other things, that an Anglican Priest working in a German Parish would not be able to Confirm. Similarly a German Pastor working in an English Parish would not normally be able to solemnize marriages recognized in English law.)*

c) The Sponsoring Body shall authorize a procedure for such appointments, involving the appropriate authorities of the two denominations and representatives of the local churches.

d) The Sponsoring Body shall determine questions of payment of ministers' salaries, pensions and expenses, and shall resolve any disputed matters concerning ministerial functions.

NOTE: *Guidelines for (c) and (d) above will be provided by the LEP Officer appointed by the Meissen Commission.*

e) The ministers shall be subject to the normal discipline of the denomination to which each belongs.

f) Newly appointed ministers shall be inducted/welcomed at a service at which they, the congregation and representatives of the Sponsoring Body shall affirm/reaffirm the Declaration of Intent.

NOTE: *The Induction or Welcome must meet the legal and liturgical requirements of the appointing authority and due account must also be taken of the full range of ecumenical relationships in which the participating churches are involved locally.*

7. Joint decision making

a) There shall be a Local Partnership Group comprising the ministers and lay representatives from each congregation in the Partnership, appointed/elected in a way approved by the Sponsoring Body. It is expected that such representatives shall be members of, or have access to, the decision making body of their congregation.

b) The Local Partnership Group shall elect a Chairperson and Secretary on an alternating basis, and shall set up such committees or working groups as it shall consider necessary.

c) The Local Partnership Group shall meet at least once a year for prayer and study, and shall consider how the partnership may be promoted and expressed in joint mission activity. The Link Officers appointed by the Sponsoring Body should always be invited to attend.

d) The Local Partnership Group shall produce an Annual Report for its constituent parishes, the Sponsoring Body and the Meissen Commission.

8. Wider participation

Other churches in or near the neighbourhood of the Partnership may negotiate for participation in the Partnership at any time; subject to the agreement of the appropriate denominational authorities and the Sponsoring Body.

NOTE: *For the Church of England see Canon B44.2(2).*

9. Review

The Sponsoring Body shall ensure that every seven years, or sooner, the Partnership shall be evaluated with reference to its objectives set out in the Declaration of Intent/Covenant Declaration and the Constitution. A copy of the Review Report should be sent to the Meissen Commission.

10. Continuity

The Partnership shall only be terminated with the approval of the appropriate denominational authorities and of the Sponsoring Body.

NOTE: *For the Church of England see Canon B44.3.*

11. Amendments

The constitution of this Partnership may be amended by the Sponsoring Body on the authority of the decision making bodies of the partner churches.

The Draft Declaration of Intent and Draft Constitution have been adapted from *Constitutional Guidelines for a Local Ecumenical Partnership,* CTE Group for Unity, 1998.

appendix H
publications

The following have been published in order to promote relationships and understanding between our Churches:

Anglo-German Ecumenical Links: an information pack from the Meissen Commission, Council for Christian Unity, new edition 1999.

The Meissen Agreement: Texts, Council for Christian Unity Occasional Paper No. 2, 1992.

Colin Podmore, *The German Evangelical Church: An Introduction following the Meissen Agreement*, Council for Christian Unity Occasional Paper No. 1, 1992.

Visible Unity and the Ministry of Oversight: The Second Theological Conference held under the Meissen Agreement, Church House Publishing, 1997.

Copies of all these publications are available from the Council for Christian Unity and the EKD Kirchenamt.

index